JESUS
meditations for the millennium

Teach me teach me dearest J,
in Thine sweet, loving, way
All the lessons of perfection
I must practice day by day

Teach me Meekness dearest J, — of thine own the envied part
not in words & actions only
But the Meekness of the heart

— Teach humility sweet Jesus
to this poor proud heart of mine
which yet wishes, oh my J—
to be modeled after Thine

Teach me fervor dearest J,
to comply with every grace
so as never to look backward
Never slacken in the race

Teach me poverty dear J.
  That my heart may never cling (waver)
  To whatever it might sever
  From my Savior, Spouse & King

Teach me chastity dear J.

  But the pureness of the heart
Teach thy heart to me dear J
  is my fervent final prayer
For all lessons & perfections
  are in full perfection There
_____

Song   Open My Eyes - hory

JESUS
meditations for the millennium

MARK LINK

ThomasMore®
– An RCL Company –

ALLEN, TEXAS

IMPRIMI POTEST
Bradley M. Schaeffer, S.J.

NIHIL OBSTAT
Rev. Msgr. Glenn D. Gardner, J.C.D.
Censor Librorum

IMPRIMATUR
† Most Rev. Charles V. Grahmann
Bishop of Dallas

January 15, 1997

The Nihil Obstat and Imprimatur are official declarations
that the material reviewed is free of doctrinal or moral
error. No implication is contained therein that those
granting the Nihil Obstat and Imprimatur agree with the
contents, opinions, or statements expressed.

Meditations for the Millennium: Jesus is adapted from *Jesus
Beyond 2000.*

ACKNOWLEDGMENT
Unless otherwise noted, all Scripture quotations are
from Today's English Version text. Copyright © American
Bible Society 1966, 1971, 1976, 1992. Used by permission.

Cover photo: Photodisc

Send all inquiries to:
Thomas More®
An RCL Company
200 East Bethany Drive
Allen, Texas 75002–3804

Toll Free   800–264–0368
Fax   800–688–8356

Vision 2000 on Internet—http://v2000.org

Printed in the United States of America

Library of Congress Catalog Card Number: 98–60987

7421   ISBN 0–88347–421–2

1 2 3 4 5   01 00 99 98

Contents

A prayer journey

In his book *Born Again,*
Charles Colson, former White House aide,
says of his relationship with his wife:

"In the ten years we'd been married,
I realized, we'd never discussed . . .
the faith deep down inside either of us."
Then he adds: "How much on the surface
are even the closest of human relationships."

Unfortunately, this is also often true
of our relationship with Jesus.

Outwardly, we are committed to Jesus.
We wear a cross about our neck.
We go to church on Sunday, and
we try to follow the teachings of Jesus.

Deep down, however, we don't know Jesus.
Why is this?

One reason is that we've never been taught
how to communicate with Jesus
in a deep, personal, prayerful way.

It's not surprising, then, that more
and more Christians today are expressing
a desire to learn how to communicate
with Jesus in an in-depth, prayerful way.
They desire to develop
a personal relationship with him.

Meditations for the Millennium: Jesus
is an attempt to address this desire.
It grew out of
not only years of praying daily,
but also of faith sharing with others
who have been doing this.

The insights and findings
gleaned from those experiences
are now set down in an orderly way
for prayer and meditation.

Hopefully, they will assist people
to set out on the most exciting journey
the human spirit can embark upon—
a prayer journey to get to know Jesus
in a more personal, prayerful way.

To seek Jesus
is the greatest of all adventures.
To find Jesus
is the greatest of all joys.
To follow Jesus
is the greatest of all achievements.

Jesus is born

The world into which Jesus was born
was a cruel world.
Human beings were sold on the auction block
to die for the entertainment of others.
Oppression was far more common
than compassion.

It was a pain-filled world.
Lepers, cripples, and the mentally ill
limped through life as best they could.
Suffering was as inevitable
as a morning sunrise
and an evening sunset.

It was an ugly world.
Exploitation of the poor and racial prejudice
were taken for granted.
They were part of the social system.

Into this world
of pain, ugliness, and cruelty,
Jesus, the Son of God, was born.
And Jesus entered into it
not as a powerful prince,
immune from many of its terrible evils,
but as a powerless peasant,
vulnerable to all of them.

And so we begin our prayer journey
by meditating on the "coming of Jesus"
into our world.

Prayer procedure

Begin each daily meditation
with the opening prayer
printed on page 176.

End each meditation by taking a minute
to record in the journal space provided
a brief review of what went on
in your mind and your heart
during the meditation.
Address all entries directly to Jesus.

Suggested daily readings

1 Jesus' birth is announced   Lk 1:26–38
2 Jesus' conception is clarified   Mt 1:18–24
3 Jesus is taken to Bethlehem   Lk 2:1–5
4 Jesus is born   Lk 2:6–20
5 Jesus is visited by magi   Mt 2:1–12
6 Jesus' life is threatened   Mt 2:13–23
7 Jesus' light continues to shine   Jn 1:1–16

Jesus' birth is foretold
to Mary by an angel

*[God sent an angel to Nazareth
to a girl named Mary.] The angel said . . .
"You will become pregnant and give birth
to a son, and you will name him Jesus. . . ."
Mary said to the angel, "I am a virgin.
How, then, can this be?" The angel answered,
"The Holy Spirit will come on you. . . ."
"I am the Lord's servant," said Mary;
"may it happen to me."* Luke 1:30–31, 34–35, 38

A young person describes hearing and saying
yes to God's call as Mary did:
"I was raised in a small town and my home
overlooked the ocean. . . . My mother would
often take me to . . . the harbor,
and would teach me to sit still and
listen to God in the wind, in the sea, in life.
She would say, 'Be quiet
and God will speak to you.'
God did speak to me, and for a long time . . .
I tried my best to run from God. . . .
I finally said 'Fiat' (So be it). . . .
At that moment my whole being filled
with a great inner peace and joy which I
shall never forget." Vincent Dwyer, *Lift Your Sails*

Have I ever felt God was speaking to me
but I did not want to follow? When? Why?

*How can I ever be content to creep after
I have felt the impulse to fly?* Anonymous

Journal

Jesus' conception
is revealed to Joseph

[Mary was betrothed to Joseph.]
An angel of the Lord appeared to him in a dream
and said, ". . . Take Mary to be your wife.
For it is by the Holy Spirit
that she has conceived.
She will have a son,
and you will name him Jesus."   Matthew 1:20–21

Jewish "betrothals"
grew out of the ancient Jewish custom
of having parents
pick marriage partners for their children.
Conceivably,
two young people did not know each other
before the period of betrothal.
The betrothal period gave them a chance
to get acquainted; it lasted about a year.
Betrothal had the force of marriage.
A groom-to-be could not renounce
his bride-to-be except by divorce.
If he died during the betrothal period,
his bride-to-be became his legal widow.
Likewise, if a bride-to-be was unfaithful
during the betrothal period,
she could be punished as an adulteress.

If I were Joseph, what would be my thoughts
before the dream? After the dream?

If you judge people,
you have no time to love them.   Mother Teresa

Jesus is taken
to the town of Bethlehem

Emperor Augustus ordered a census
to be taken throughout the Roman Empire. . . .
Everyone, then, went to register . . . ,
each to his own hometown.
Joseph went . . . to the town of Bethlehem . . .
the birthplace of King David . . .
because he was a descendant of David.
He went . . . with Mary.   Luke 2:1, 3–5

During the reign of Emperor Augustus,
a widespread feeling of expectation
began to stir among the masses in both
Rome and Judea. "It was often associated
with the figure of a 'savior' or deliverer . . .
with something of divinity about him.
Millions . . . saw the emperor himself
as the divine deliverer."   C. H. Dodd   But when
Augustus died, so did the Roman expectancy.
Unlike the expectancy of the Roman masses,
the Jews could pinpoint the reason
for their expectancy.
Their prophets of old had foretold
the coming of a glorious king,
a descendant of David.
To this king was given the title "Messiah."

What kind of effect do I think the angelic
appearances to Mary and Joseph had on their
thinking as they traveled to Bethlehem?

"Do not be afraid."   Joshua 1:9

Journal

Jesus is born in Bethlehem

While they were in Bethlehem,
the time came for Mary to have her baby.
She . . . wrapped him in cloths and
laid him in a manger—there was no room
for them to stay in the inn.   Luke 2:6–7

Sister Mary Coleman, a Maryknoll nun,
spent a good part of World War II in a
Japanese prison camp in the Philippines.
The prisoners set up a prayer room.
One of the Filipinos carved a wooden
crucifix and it was hung on the wall.
It proved to be a great aid to prayer.
When Christmas came, several prisoners
carved crib figures for the prayer room.
A guard who had watched the prisoners
meditate before the crucifix
now watched them do so with equal fervor
before the baby Jesus.
One day he pointed to the crib and then
to the crucifix. He asked, "Same person?"
Sister Coleman said softly, "Same person."
Then he said with deep feeling, "I'm sorry."

This story makes several points.
Which strikes me most and why?

O Christmas Sun!
What holy task is thine!
To fold a world in the embrace of God.
                                    Guy Wetmore Carryl

Jesus is visited by wise men from the East

*Some men who studied the stars
came from the East to Jerusalem and asked,
"Where is the baby born to be the king
of the Jews? We saw his star . . . and
we have come to worship him."*   Matthew 2:1–2

The whole world watched as *Apollo 11*
splashed down in the Pacific on July 20, 1969,
after putting the first human on the moon.
Later, the *Apollo 11* crew of Armstrong,
Collins, and Aldrin went on a 23-nation tour.
Aldrin said of their visit to the Vatican:
"It turned out to be one of the most striking
and stirring moments of the trip when His
Holiness Pope Paul VI, a frail, worn man . . .
unveiled three magnificent porcelain
statues of the Three Wise Men.
He said that these three men were directed
to the infant Christ by looking at the stars
and that we three also reached
our destination by looking at the stars."

What do I find to be the greatest help
in directing me and keeping me on course
in my journey to Jesus and eternal life?

*A French atheist told a farmer,
"We'll pull down every church steeple
to destroy your superstitions."
"Perhaps," said the farmer,
"but you can't help leaving us the stars."*

13

Journal

Jesus' life is threatened by Herod

*After the wise men had left, an angel . . .
appeared in a dream to Joseph and said,
"Herod will be looking for the child
in order to kill him. . . . Take the child
and his mother and escape to Egypt."
[Joseph did as the angel said.]*   Matthew 2:13

Kathryn Koob was one 54 Americans
taken hostage by Shiite extremists
in Iran in 1979 and held for 444 days.
On Christmas of 1980 her captors
paraded her before the world on TV,
letting her send greetings to her family.
She turned the situation into a movingly
spiritual experience by singing a carol
she had learned as a child:
"Away in a manger, no crib for a bed,
the little Lord Jesus
laid down his sweet head. . . .
Bless all the dear children
in thy tender care,
And fit us for heaven to live with thee there."

Herod's violence and Iranian terrorism
marred the beauty of Christmas
but could not destroy it. What are some
early Christmas memories that I have?

*The star of Bethlehem
is a star in the darkness of night
even today.*   Edith Stein

Jesus' light continues to shine in the darkness

*The light shines in the darkness, and
the darkness has never put it out.*   John 1:5

Austrian psychotherapist Victor Frankl
was a prisoner in a Nazi concentration camp.
In *Man's Search for Meaning,* he recalls
digging a trench on a cold winter morning:
"Gray was the sky above;
gray the snow in the pale light of dawn;
gray the rags in which my fellow prisoners
were clad, and gray their faces. . . .
I was struggling
to find a reason for my sufferings. . . .
In a last violent protest against
the hopelessness of imminent death,
I sensed my spirit . . .
say 'Yes' in answer to my question
of the existence of ultimate purpose.
At that moment a light was lit in a distant
farmhouse, which stood on the horizon . . .
in the mist of the miserable gray
of a dawning morning in Bavaria."

Have I ever wondered about the purpose
of my own life? What is its purpose?

*You yourselves used to be in the darkness,
but since you have become the Lord's people,
you are in the light.
So you must live like people
who belong to the light.*   Ephesians 5:8

Jesus is baptized

*Each newborn child arrives on earth
with a message to deliver to mankind.
Clenched in his little fist
is some particle of yet unrevealed truth,
some missing clue, which may solve
the enigma of man's destiny. . . . He must
be treated as top-sacred.*   Sam Levinson

If any newborn child was "top-sacred,"
it was John the Baptist. His story began
when an angel appeared to Zechariah
and said, "Your wife Elizabeth
will bear you a son."   Luke 1:13

Zechariah was doubtful, saying, "I am an
old man, and my wife is old also."   Luke 1:18
The angel said,
"Because you have not believed,
you will be unable to speak . . .
until the day [your son is born]."   Luke 1:20

When John was born,
Zechariah regained his speech.

*Everyone who heard of it
thought about it and asked,
"What is this child going to be?"
For it was plain
that the Lord's power was upon him.*   Luke 1:66

Filled with the Holy Spirit,
Zechariah said to his newborn son:

*"You, my child, will be called
a prophet of the Most High God.
You will go ahead of the Lord
to prepare his road for him." . . .*

*John grew and . . . lived in the desert
until the day when he appeared publicly
to the people of Israel.*   Luke 1:76, 80

This week's meditations focus on
John the Baptist,
who "prepared the road" for Jesus.

Suggested daily readings

1 John appears   Mt 3:1–6

2 John begins preaching   Jn 1:19–28

3 John baptizes Jesus   Mt 3:13–17

4 John speaks about Jesus   Jn 3:22–35

5 John identifies Jesus   Jn 1:29–34

6 Jesus confronts Satan   Mt 4:1–11

7 Jesus eulogizes John   Mt 11:1–11

Jesus' mission is previewed by John

*[One day John the Baptist appeared
at the Jordan preaching to the people.]
"Turn away from your sins," he said. . . .
"The Kingdom of heaven is near!"* Matthew 3:2

Dennis Alessi was walking down
a busy street in downtown Baltimore.
At an intersection stood an elderly man
calling out to the passersby,
"Turn away from sin. Turn back to God!"
His pulpit was a clean metal trash can.
He was bald, wore glasses,
and was neatly dressed. Dennis said later:
"His pleas were dignified and sincere. . . .
I had no idea whether that man calling
into the crowd was heard by one
or a hundred others.
But he reached something in me. . . .
[I was moved to return] to the Church,
from which I'd been absent for seven years."
"The Open Door," *Catholic Digest* (Feb. 1996)

How do I explain the impact of this modern
"John the Baptist" on Dennis?
How relevant is his message for our day?

*"Listen! I stand at the door and knock;
if any hear my voice and open the door,
I will come into their house
and eat with them,
and they will eat with me."* Revelation 3:20

Journal

17

Journal

Jesus' path
is made straight by John

[People began asking John, "Who are you?"
He said,] "I am 'the voice of someone
shouting . . . Make a straight path
for the Lord to travel!'"   John 1:23

General Charles Gordon
was admired by all who knew him.
When England proposed to honor him
with money and titles, he refused.
He did agree, however,
to accept a lone gold medal
with a brief inscription etched on it.
After Gordon's death in 1885,
the medal could not be found anywhere.
It was later learned
that Gordon had melted the medal down,
sold the gold, and given the cash to the poor.
On the date of the gift, his diary reads:
"The last earthly thing I had in this world
that I valued, I have given to the Lord."

How is Gordon's action a perfect response
to what John had in mind when he preached,
"Make a straight path for the Lord"?
What is one concrete action I might take
in response to John's message?

When the soul has laid down its faults
at the feet of God,
it feels as though it had wings.
                    Eugenie de Guerin

Jesus is baptized
by a reluctant John

Journal

[One day Jesus came to John for baptism.
John said,] "I ought to be baptized by you. . . ."
Jesus said, "Let it be so for now."

Matthew 3:14–15

John had told people to be baptized
as a sign of their commitment
to turn from sin and back to God.
This raises a question:
Why was the sinless Jesus baptized?
By becoming one of us, Jesus became
a member of our sinful human family.
He would not separate himself from us—
even in our sinfulness.
Thus, he teaches us an important lesson.
We cannot separate ourselves
from our sinful human family either,
especially from its "family" sins:
disregard for the poor,
disrespect for life in all forms,
discrimination against human differences.

How do such "family" sins affect me?
Do they tend to depress or challenge me?
If Jesus died because of our "family" sins,
what ought I to do about them?

The only thing needed
for evil to triumph in today's world
is for good people to do nothing.
Edmund Burke (slightly adapted)

Journal

Jesus is the "groom"; John is the "best man"

*[John the Baptist compared his relationship
with Jesus to that of a best man
to a bridegroom. He said of Jesus,]
"He must become more important
while I become less important."*   John 3:30

In Jewish weddings, the best man
supervised the wedding invitations
and orchestrated the wedding celebration.
His final job was to keep vigil at the
bridal chamber until the groom arrived.
Once the groom arrived, his job was over
and he withdrew from the limelight.
This is what John the Baptist did.
He took charge of the wedding of Israel
(the bride) to Jesus (the bridegroom).
Jesus used wedding imagery, also,
to explain why his disciples did not fast.
He said, "As long as the bridegroom
is with them, they will not do that."   Mark 2:19

How gracefully do I step from the limelight,
as John the Baptist did, when this is
the appropriate or proper thing to do?

*God in heaven,
let me feel my nothingness,
not in order to despair over it,
but in order to feel the more powerfully
the greatness of your goodness.*
Soren Kierkegaard

Jesus is identified as the "Lamb of God"

The next day . . . [when John saw Jesus,
he said to two friends,]
"There is the Lamb of God,
who takes away the sin of the world!
This is the one I was talking about."
                                    John 1:29–30

Harvey Mackay knows business inside out.
He calls Billy Graham the best salesman
he's ever met. What makes him remarkable,
Mackay says, is that he sells a product that
nobody has ever seen—eternal salvation.
What makes Billy even more remarkable,
says Mackay, is his mediocre style.
His delivery is pedestrian,
he's not entertaining or funny, and
he doesn't claim to be a great Bible scholar.
Why is Billy the best? Mackay answers,
"His dedication to his 'customers.'
Every action he takes is designed to meet
their needs, not his own. And it shows."

John was like that. His dedication was total.
Every action was designed to meet the needs
of the people: to prepare them
to open their hearts to Jesus' salvation.
How dedicated am I to my "mission" in life?

I heard the Lord say,
"Whom shall I send? . . ."
I answered, "I will go! Send me!"   Isaiah 6:8

Journal

Jesus is led by the Spirit into the desert

*Then the Spirit led Jesus into the desert
to be tempted by the Devil. After spending
forty days and nights without food,
Jesus was hungry. Then the Devil came
to him and said, "If you are God's Son,
order these stones to turn into bread."
But Jesus answered, "The scripture says,
'[You] cannot live on bread alone.'"*   Matthew 4:1–4

Howard LaFay says that during Holy Week
in Andalusia (southern Spain),
"Everyone appears in their finest,
even the poorest households produce
a few bouquets. . . . For most of my life
I shared the stern Anglo-Saxon disapproval
of decking statues with silk and jewels
while people struggled for daily bread.
But after [Holy Week] . . . in Andalusia,
I am no longer sure. For this short,
shining season, God's poor live amid
blossoms and brocade, gold and lace.
For an octave of days they lose themselves
in a vision of glory and redemption.
Against this, what is bread?"
National Geographic (June 1975)

How do I answer LaFay's question?

*I feel sorry for the person who has never
gone without a meal to buy a ticket
to a concert.*   Albert Wiggam (slightly adapted)

Jesus eulogizes John the Baptist

[Just before John was beheaded by Herod, Jesus eulogized him, saying,]
"John the Baptist is greater than anyone who has ever lived."   Matthew 11:11

Charlie Ross was President Truman's
close friend and press secretary.
When Ross died suddenly,
the grief-stricken president wrote out
in long hand a eulogy
that he was to read at a press conference.
It began: "The friend of my youth,
who became a tower of strength
when the responsibilities of high office
so unexpectedly fell to me, is gone."
At this point in the eulogy, Truman choked.
He said, "Ah hell, I can't read this thing.
You fellows know how I feel anyway."
With tears in his eyes,
he gave them the handwritten eulogy
and walked sobbing to his office.

It was this kind of love that Jesus held
for John the Baptist.
Is there a close friend or associate
to whom I owe a great deal and ought to
express my appreciation now—rather than
wait and eulogize the person at death?

The finger of God touches your life
when you make a friend.   Mary Dawson Hughes

Jesus starts his mission

One day Jesus was walking
along the beach of the Sea of Galilee.
He came upon two fishermen,
Simon and his brother Andrew,
casting their nets for fish.
He said to them:

"Come with me,
and I will teach you to catch people."
At once they left their nets
and went with him.   Mark 1:17–18

This same gospel scene
repeats itself over and over in our times.
The same Jesus
who walked in people's midst
along the seashore
continues to walk in people's midst
along our streets.

The Jesus who called to Simon
and Andrew is the same Jesus
who calls out to people today.

And the invitation he extended
to Simon and Andrew is the same one
he extends to people today:
"Come follow me!"

The response
of Simon and Andrew to that invitation
changed their lives forever.

In a similar way our response to it
will change our lives forever.

Prayer procedure

Be sure to begin each meditation with
the opening prayer (see page 176)
and to end it with the Lord's Prayer.
These two prayers
function as a focus and a framework
for each meditation session.

Suggested daily readings

1 Jesus chooses the apostles   Lk 6:12–19
2 Jesus chooses Peter   Mt 16:13–20
3 Jesus says, "Fear not!"   Mt 10:26–31
4 Jesus warns his apostles   Mt 10:16–25
5 Jesus tours towns   Lk 8:1–8
6 Jesus pities the people   Mt 9:35–38
7 Jesus calls Levi   Mk 2:13–17

Jesus chooses
twelve apostles

[Jesus chose Simon and Andrew,]
James and John, Philip and Bartholomew,
Matthew and Thomas, James son of Alphaeus,
and Simon (. . . the Patriot), Judas
son of James, and Judas Iscariot.   Luke 6:14–16

To: Jesus of Nazareth
From: Jerusalem Business Consultants, Inc.
We have reviewed the resumés
of your candidates for managerial posts.
We recommend you continue your search.
Peter is too emotional and prone
to faulty snap judgments.   Luke 22:33
James and John lack a team spirit and are
prone to be hotheads.   Matthew 20:20–21, Luke 9:54
Thomas will miss meetings and is a skeptic.
Simon is a left-wing political zealot
who would fight constantly with Matthew,
an establishment tax collector,
currently under investigation by our bureau.
The only candidate you should retain
is the highly motivated and competitive
Judas Iscariot.   (Inspired by similar accounts)

What do I think Jesus was looking for most
in those he chose to be his twelve apostles?

The LORD said . . .
"I do not judge as people judge.
They look at the outward appearance,
but I look at the heart."   1 Samuel 16:7

Journal

_____

_____

_____

_____

_____

_____

_____

_____

_____

_____

_____

Jesus gives Peter the keys of the Kingdom

Jesus said, "Peter: you are a rock,
and on this rock foundation
I will build my church. . . .
I will give you
the keys of the Kingdom of heaven;
what you prohibit on earth
will be prohibited in heaven,
and what you permit on earth
will be permitted in heaven."   Matthew 16:18–19

Michelangelo was hired by Pope Paul III
to paint the *Last Judgment* in the Vatican.
As it neared completion,
a minor papal official kept pestering
the artist for a private sneak preview of it.
His patience at an end, Michelangelo decided
to teach the minor official a lesson.
He painted him among the sinners
being punished in hell.
When the official learned about his fate,
he complained to the pope, who said,
"As Peter's successor,
Jesus gave me the authority to prohibit
and to permit on earth and in heaven,
but he said nothing of authority over hell.
I'm afraid the matter is out of my hands."

How do I react to slights or humiliations?

He who stays not in his littleness
loses his greatness.   Saint Francis de Sales

Jesus instructs the apostles in how to preach

Jesus said,
"What I am telling you in the dark
you must repeat in broad daylight,
and what you have heard in private
you must announce from the housetops."
Matthew 10:27

A church property lay at a busy crossing.
Hardly five minutes passed
without drivers sitting in idling cars,
waiting for the light to turn green.
One day a parishioner got an idea
not only for lessening their boredom
but also for spreading the Gospel.
A sign was built to provide both
entertainment and "food for thought."
Each week a thought appears on it,
such as: "Your seat in eternity:
Will it be smoking or nonsmoking?" Anonymous
"If God loved us as much as we love God,
where would we all be?" Anonymous
"Feeding the hungry is greater work
than raising the dead." Saint John Chrysostom

Can I think of a way we might preach
God's word more creatively? How?

Discovery consists
in seeing what everyone has seen
and thinking what nobody has thought.
Albert Szent-Gyorgyi

Journal

_____

_____

_____

_____

_____

_____

_____

_____

_____

_____

_____

27

Jesus sends out
the twelve apostles

[Jesus said to his twelve apostles,]
"I am sending you out
just like sheep to a pack of wolves.
You must be as cautious as snakes
and as gentle as doves. . . .
Everyone will hate you because of me.
But whoever holds out to the end
will be saved."   Matthew 10:16, 22

Voltaire was a French philosopher and wit.
Often in trouble with authorities,
he was exiled to England in the early 1700s.
At that time anti-French feelings ran high.
One day Voltaire was surrounded
by an angry mob in London
that kept shouting, "Hang the Frenchman!"
Pleading for silence, Voltaire
cried out, theatrically, "Men of England!
You wish to kill me because I am French.
Has not the good God punished me enough
by not creating me to be an Englishman?"
The mob roared hysterically with laughter,
cheered Voltaire, and
escorted him safely back to his dwelling.

How well do I keep my cool and respond
diplomatically when people say things
that make me fighting mad?

Anger is the wind that blows out
the lamp of the mind.   Robert Ingersoll

Jesus preaches in towns and villages

Journal

Jesus traveled through towns and villages,
preaching . . . about the Kingdom of God.
The twelve disciples went with him,
and so did some women . . . who used
their own resources to help.   Luke 8:1–3

Young Samuel Clemens (Mark Twain)
was returning home one night.
He saw what looked like a page from a book
blowing along the sidewalk.
Catching up with it, he saw it was a page
from a story about a certain Joan of Arc.
He'd never heard of her, but reading the page
gave him a deep compassion for her.
Years later he wrote
Personal Recollections of Joan of Arc.
It was called "the loveliest story" ever
written about the martyred peasant girl.
Her holiness and valor revitalized
the morale of the French army and changed
the course of European history.

What are my thoughts about God's choice
of unlikely people, like a peasant girl,
to play such a key role in history?

God selects his own instruments,
and sometimes they are queer ones;
for instance, he chose me
to steer the ship through a great crisis.
Abraham Lincoln

29

Journal

Jesus' heart is filled with pity

[Jesus went about teaching the people.]
As he saw the crowds,
his heart was filled pity . . .
because they were . . . like sheep
without a shepherd.
So he said to his disciples,
"The harvest is large, but there are
few workers to gather it in." Matthew 9:36–37

Sherry Lansing is the most powerful woman
in the movie industry. She is chairwoman
of Paramount Pictures and has worked
on such classic films as *Chariots of Fire,*
The China Syndrome, and *Fatal Attraction.*
Sherry credits her mother for her success.
After Sherry's dad died of a heart attack,
her mother took over the family business.
Sherry still remembers an office manager
saying to her mother, "But you can't do this.
You know nothing about the business."
Her mother said, "I can do it! Teach me."

People in Jesus' time—and people today—
hunger for Jesus' message of hope,
but there are few willing to teach them.
How do I explain the unwillingness of people
to teach others about this message?
How willing am I?

Jesus said,
"Listen, then, if you have ears!" Mark 4:23

Jesus' call of Levi the tax collector

Jesus saw a tax collector,
Levi son of Alphaeus, sitting in his office.
Jesus said to him, "Follow me."
Levi got up and followed him.   Mark 2:14

Presidential aide Charles Colson
was imprisoned in the Watergate scandal.
Out of his prison experience
grew his present ministry to prisoners.
In *Born Again,*
he tells how it all took shape in his mind.
One day he thought to himself:
"Just as God felt it necessary
to become man to help His children,
could it be that I had become a prisoner
to better understand [prison life]? . . .
Could I ever understand the horrors
of prison life by visiting a prison? . . .
Of course not. . . .
For the rest of my life I would know and feel
what it is like to be imprisoned, the steady,
gradual corrosion of a man's soul. . . .
Out of these startling thoughts
came the beginning of a revelation—
that I was being given a prison ministry."

How do I experience Jesus calling me
to follow him more closely—right now?

Since you have accepted Christ Jesus . . .
build your lives on him.   Colossians 2:6–7

31

Miracles are revelations

One day Jesus drove a demon out of a man.
Most people were amazed. But some said,
"The chief of the demons . . . gives him
the power to drive them out."   Luke 11:15

Jesus replied, "No, it is rather by means
of God's power that I drive out demons."

Then Jesus added something very important.
He said, "This proves that the Kingdom of God
has already come to you."   Luke 11:20

And so the *first* thing Jesus' miracles did
was to reveal the arrival of God's Kingdom.

Besides driving out evil spirits,
Jesus also restored sight to the blind,
hearing to the deaf, and health to the lame.

When some disciples of John the Baptist
saw this, they asked Jesus if he were
the "promised one." Jesus replied,
"The blind can see, the lame can walk . . .
[and] the deaf can hear."   Luke 7:22

Jesus' reply makes it clear
that his miracles make present the "signs"
that the prophets said would signal
the arrival of the promised Messiah:
"The blind will be able to see,
and the deaf will hear.
The lame will leap and dance."   Isaiah 35:5–6

And so the *second* thing Jesus' miracles did
was to reveal the arrival of the Messiah.
Jesus is the "promised one."

This week's meditations focus on
two important things about miracles.

First, Jesus used them to reveal the arrival
of God's *Kingdom* and God's *Messiah*.

Second, Jesus still uses them today
to reveal to us
important things about our personal lives.

Suggested daily readings

1 Jesus heals the sick   Mk 6:53–56

2 Jesus heals a leper   Mt 8:1–4

3 Jesus heals a blind man   Mk 8:22–25

4 Jesus heals a deaf-mute   Mk 7:31–37

5 Jesus heals two blind men   Mt 9:27–31

6 Jesus feeds a crowd   Mk 8:1–10

7 Jesus heals and preaches   Mt 11:1–6

Jesus heals all
who touch him

*People would take their sick
to the marketplaces and beg Jesus to let
the sick at least touch the edge of his cloak.
And all who touched it were made well.*
Mark 6:56

England was involved in the Crimean War
in Russia from 1845 to 1856.
The wounded were laid side by side
in makeshift hospitals that were dirty,
overcrowded, and understaffed.
The wind blew the stench from open sewers,
making breathing difficult. Rats ran wild.
Into this incredible, hopeless situation
came Florence Nightingale
and 38 nurses she had trained in England.
Sometimes she spent 20 hours straight
on her feet, directing sanitation efforts
and bandaging the wounded.
The bedridden soldiers worshiped her
and would "kiss her shadow
as it fell across their pillows."

If the sick and the needy are to
experience Jesus' healing presence today,
it must be through loving, caring people.
How ready am I to be the healing presence
of Jesus in today's world?

*Blessed is the influence of one, true,
loving human soul on another.*   George Eliot

Journal

Jesus touches
and heals a leper

[A leper approached Jesus and said,]
"Sir, if you want to, you can make me clean."
Jesus reached out and touched him.
"I do want to," he answered. "Be clean!"
At once the man was healed.   Matthew 8:1–3

Evidence is mounting
to show that when hands are placed
on sick people with a desire to heal them,
their recovery rate improves.
One explanation for this amazing fact is
that the loving touch of loving people
releases within a sick person
an energy that promotes healing.
If this explanation is correct,
and if Jesus is God, and if God is love—
infinite love—then the touch of Jesus
could not help but release in a person
an enormous healing energy.
It would have been a "miracle" had
the people he touched *not* been healed.

How easily do I reach out in a loving way
to pat the head of a sick person,
to wipe the tears of a child,
to show affection for a family member?

God said, "My saving power
will rise on you like the sun
and bring healing like the sun's rays."
Malachi 4:2

Jesus touches and heals a blind person

Journal

*[One day Jesus placed his hands
on a blind man and asked,]
"Can you see anything?"
The man looked up and said,
"Yes, I can see people, but they look like trees
walking around." Jesus again placed his hands
on the man's eyes. This time . . .
he saw everything clearly.*   Mark 8:22–25

In his book *The Christian Vision,*
John Powell tells of meeting a young man
who grew up unable to see objects
even just a few feet from his eyes.
His parents were poor and uneducated
and did not seek help for him.
When he was eighteen, the young man
went to an eye doctor for the first time.
After fitting the young man with lenses,
the doctor told him to look out the window.
"Wow!" the young man exclaimed.
"This is incredible, absolutely incredible.
I can't believe how beautiful everything is!"

Helen Keller, who was blind, said,
"The greatest calamity . . . is to have sight
and fail to see." Do I have a "blindness"
from which I need Jesus to heal me?
What is it?

*The real voyage of discovery consists . . .
in seeing with new eyes.*   Marcel Proust

Journal

Jesus touches
and heals a deaf-mute

*Some people brought Jesus a man
who was deaf and could hardly speak. . . .
[Jesus touched the man and said,]*
"Ephphatha," *which means, "Open up!"
At once the man was able to hear . . .
and he began to talk without any trouble.*
Mark 7:32, 34–35

Helen Keller was blind, deaf, and dumb.
In *The Story of My Life* she tells how
Miss Fuller taught her how to talk:
"She passed my hand lightly over her face,
and let me feel the position of her tongue
and lips when she made a sound. . . .
I labored night and day. . . .
My work was practice, practice, practice. . . .
I used to repeat ecstatically,
"I am not dumb now." . . .
My mother pressed me close. . . .
Mildred seized my free hand and kissed it
and danced, and my father expressed
his pride and affection in a big silence."

Do I have some kind of inability to "speak"
or "hear" that I would like Jesus
to heal in me? What is it?

*The chief exercise of prayer
is to speak to God
and to hear God speak to you
in the depths of your heart.* Saint Francis de Sales

Jesus touches
and heals two blind people

[Two blind people were following Jesus.]
"Have mercy on us, Son of David!"
they shouted. . . .
Then Jesus touched their eyes . . .
and their sight was restored.

Matthew 9:27, 29–30

Abraham Lincoln and Gilbert Greene
were walking outside of town one night.
Greene described what happened:
"As we walked on the country road . . .
Lincoln turned his eyes to the heavens
full of stars, and told me their names. . . .
He said, 'I never behold them
that I do not feel
that I am looking in the face of God.
I can see how it might be possible
for a man to look down upon earth
and be an atheist,
but I cannot conceive
how he could look up into the heavens
and say there is no God.'"

Emanuel Hertz, ed., *Lincoln Talks: A Biography in Anecdote*

How blind am I to God's presence and God's
wisdom shining forth from our world?

He has decided the number of the stars
and calls each one by name.
Great and mighty is our Lord;
his wisdom cannot be measured.   Psalms 147:4–5

Journal

37

Journal

Jesus feeds
a hungry crowd

*Jesus ordered the crowd to sit down
on the ground. Then he took seven loaves
[and] gave thanks to God. . . . Everybody ate
and had enough—there were about four
thousand people.*   Mark 8:6, 8

Walter Petrvage grew up in a small town
in Pennsylvania. Among his fond memories
is his father's deep compassion.
For example, on the night of the senior prom
he took his father's car without permission.
In his rush to get away without detection,
he left the driver's door slightly open
to check clearance
as he backed out of the narrow garage.
The door hit the garage, springing the hinges.
He laid awake most of the night worrying.
When he came downstairs about noon,
his dad said, "I took the Chevy to the body shop.
They'll have it fixed tomorrow.
We can decided who'll pay for it then."
He paused and then said, "Did you have
a good time at the prom?"   *Catholic Digest* (June 1996)

How compassionate am I—as Jesus was
to the crowd and the father to his son?

*You may call God love,
you may call God goodness.
But the best name for God is compassion.*
                                        Meister Eckhart

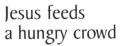

Jesus heals the deaf and preaches to the poor

Journal

*Jesus said, "The deaf hear . . . and
the Good News is preached to the poor."*
                                    Matthew 11:5

A mother found a note written by her child,
who was deaf. It went something like this:
"Dear God: I don't want to hurt your feelings,
but I wish you hadn't made me deaf.
Could you change me back. [signed] Sue.
P.S. Say hello to my guardian angel."
Next day, Sue found a note. It was written
in gold ink and went something like this:
"Dear Sue:
I am your guardian angel, and I asked God
to answer your note. You see,
God made me deaf, too. But God did give me
two fast legs, so I can run like the wind;
two lovely arms, so I can hug everybody;
and an imagination, so I can fly anywhere.
What I really like most, however,
is being able to turn off my hearing aid
when the other angels are yelling.
It makes things quiet so I can better hear God
singing love songs to me in my heart.
[signed] Your guardian angel.
P.S. We love more and more every day!"

What is the point of the angel's letter?

*Faith knows the way; hope points the way.
Love is the way.*   Anonymous

Miracles are invitations

The novel *Father Malachy's Miracle*
was made into a play.
It is a fanciful story of a priest in Scotland
who gets the idea of praying for a miracle
so powerful that it will leave no doubt
about the truthfulness of God and religion.

"One spectacular miracle," he tells a friend,
"and we shall prove to the world . . .
that we have the Light and the truth."

And so he prays that on a certain night
an evil nightclub will take flight and
be carried off to a barren island
off Scotland's coast.

The miracle takes place. But it backfires.
Instead of convincing people of the truth,
it is turned into a big publicity stunt
by the nightclub's owner.

The story ends
with a wiser Father Malachy realizing
that you can't make people believe.
You can only invite them
to open their hearts to the gift of faith.

This brings us
to the second point about miracles.
Besides acting as *revelations*
of the Messiah and God's Kingdom,
they also serve as *invitations* to open
our hearts to the Messiah and the Kingdom.
How so?

The healing of blind people invites us
to open our eyes to Jesus' works.
The healing of deaf people invites us
to open our ears to Jesus' words.
And the raising of dead people invites us
to be reborn and begin living new lives
in God's Kingdom.

And so this week's meditations focus on
the miracles of Jesus and
how God can use these same miracles today
to speak to each of us in a personal way.

Suggested daily readings

1	Jesus heals many sick people	Mk 3:7–12
2	Jesus cures ten lepers	Lk 17:11–19
3	Jesus heals a blind person	Lk 18:35–43
4	Jesus expels an evil spirit	Mk 1:21–28
5	Jesus heals a man's servant	Mt 8:9–13
6	Jesus walks on water	Jn 6:16–21
7	Jesus calms a storm	Mk 4:35–41

Jesus touches and heals many sick people

The sick kept pushing their way to Jesus in order to touch him.   Mark 3:10

Alexis Carrel was a Nobel prize winner
and an unbelieving French surgeon.
Then he saw a girl healed before his eyes
at the shrine of Lourdes in France.
He was stunned, unable to think.
Later, he and two other doctors examined
the girl and agreed she was totally healed.
But he still had "intellectual doubts."
That night he went for a long walk to think
things out. Later he wrote (in the third
person) in his book *The Voyage to Lourdes:*
"Back in the hotel . . .
he took the big green notebook from his bag
and sat down to write his observations. . . .
It was now three o'clock. . . .
A new coolness penetrated the open window.
He felt the serenity of nature enter his soul.
All intellectual doubts vanished."
Carrel went on to become a deeply
committed Christian the rest of his life.

Why do/don't I find it hard to accept Jesus'
invitation to believe with all my heart?

*A miracle . . . strengthens faith.
But faith in God is less apt
to proceed from miracles
than miracles from faith in God.*   Frederick Buechner

Journal

Jesus heals
a Samaritan leper

[One day Jesus cured ten lepers.
Only a Samaritan returned to thank him.
Jesus said,]
"Why is this foreigner the only one
who came back to give thanks to God?"
And Jesus said to him . . .
"Your faith has made you well."   Luke 17:18–19

Many prisoners of war collapsed under
the terror of Nazi death camps, but not all.
Psychotherapist Victor Frankl—
a prisoner himself—probed for the reason.
He concluded that the difference was faith.
Faith put some prisoners in touch with a power
that helped them maintain their humanity.
When freedom came,
some prisoners reacted bitterly;
others reacted gratefully.
Frankl was among the latter.
Shortly after his release, he was walking
through a field of wildflowers.
Overhead birds were circling and singing.
Instinctively Frankl knelt and prayed.
To this day, he has no idea how long
he knelt in prayer among the flowers.

How do I react to difficult situations?
How do they affect my faith in God?

When we do what we can,
God will do what we can't.   E. C. McKenzie

Jesus heals
a blind person

*[A blind person heard Jesus passing by
and cried out,] "Jesus! Son of David!
Have mercy on me!" . . .
Jesus stopped and . . . asked . . .
"What do you want me to do for you?"
"Sir," he answered, "I want to see again."*
Luke 18:38, 40–41

Laura Bridgman was blind, deaf, and mute.
She was the first person to educate herself
by the raised-alphabet system of Dr. Howe
of the Perkins Institute for the Blind.
Louis Braille was blinded at age three.
He went on to become a teacher and
the inventor of the Braille system
of writing for the blind.
James Thurber lost the sight of one eye
early in life and the sight of his other eye
as he grew older.
Yet he kept writing and drawing cartoons
with the aid of a large magnifying glass—
until his sight vanished completely.

What keeps me from believing
that if I open my heart to Jesus, he can
work miracles in and through me, also?

*It gives me a deep comforting sense
that things seen are temporal
and that things unseen are eternal.*
Helen Keller

Journal

Jesus expels
an evil spirit

*[One Sabbath a man with an evil spirit
came into the synagogue at Capernaum.
Seeing Jesus he screamed,] "I know
who you are—you are God's holy messenger!"
Jesus ordered the spirit,
"Be quiet, and come out of the man!"
[The spirit obeyed.]* Mark 1:24–25

An old Jewish legend describes a visit
of the Roman emperor to Rabbi Joshua.
The emperor demanded to see the "Holy One,
the Most High of Israel."
Rabbi Joshua shook his head: "Impossible!"
The emperor said, "No excuses!"
The rabbi escorted the emperor outside.
As they stood in the blinding sunlight,
the rabbi said to the emperor,
"Gaze on the face of the sun for a minute."
The emperor replied, "Impossible!"
Rabbi Joshua replied, "If it is impossible
for you to gaze on the face of the sun—
the lowly servant of the Holy One—
by what logic do you expect to gaze
on the face of the Holy One?"

Why would the evil spirit "see" the real
Jesus, when many people could not?
What keeps me from seeing Jesus better?

*True spiritual vision is the ability
to see the invisible.* Anonymous

Jesus praises
a Roman officer's faith

*[When Jesus offered
to go to the home of a Roman officer
to heal his servant, the officer said,]
"Just give the order,
and my servant will get well. . . ."
When Jesus heard this, he was surprised
and said to the people . . . "I tell you,
I have never found anyone in Israel
with faith like this."* Matthew 8:8, 10

Alexander the Great headed up
the largest empire ever ruled by one man.
According to an ancient story,
he became gravely ill one day and called
a doctor who had attended him for years.
Just before the doctor arrived,
Alexander was handed a note warning him
the doctor had been bribed to poison him.
When the doctor arrived, he poured out
a liquid for Alexander to drink.
After drinking it,
Alexander gave the note to the doctor.
It was an incredible gesture of faith.

Jesus' words and Alexander's faith
invite me to inventory my faith—
not in a doctor, but in God's own Son.
How can I strengthen it?

It is love that makes faith, not faith love.
John Henry Newman

Journal

_____

_____

_____

_____

_____

_____

_____

_____

_____

_____

_____

Jesus walks
across a stormy sea

[The disciples were on the lake in a storm.
Suddenly,] they saw Jesus
walking on the water, coming near the boat,
and they were terrified.
"Don't be afraid," Jesus told them,
"it is I!" John 6:19–20

A duck hunter bought a retriever.
He was amazed when he saw the dog
retrieve a duck by simply
running across the water of the lake.
Thirty minutes later,
his hunting partner joined him—
just as another duck flew over the lake.
The hunter fired; the duck fell;
the dog ran across the water and got it.
This happened several more times,
but the hunting partner made no comment.
Finally, the hunter said to his partner,
"Did you notice anything about that dog?"
"I certainly did," said his partner.
"He can't swim."

When it comes to the amazing things
that Jesus did,
how and why are many people like
the hunter's partner in the story?

We see things
not as they are, but as we are.
H. M. Tomlinson

Jesus calms
stormy winds and waves

Journal

[Jesus and his disciples were at sea.]
Suddenly a strong wind blew up, and the
waves began to spill over into the boat. . . .
Jesus was . . . sleeping. . . . The disciples
woke him up and said, "Teacher,
don't you care that we are about to die?"
Jesus stood up and commanded the wind,
"Be quiet!" and he said to the waves,
"Be still!" The wind died down,
and there was a great calm.   Mark 4:37–39

Lord of the wind and waves,
calm our storm when we are afraid.
Lord of the loaves and fishes,
be our food when we are hungry.
Lord of the lambs and flocks,
seek us out when we are lost.
Lord of signs and wonders,
show yourself when we have doubts.
Lord of the blind and lame,
take our hand when we falter.
Lord of the fields and flowers,
care for us when others don't.
Lord of all that lives, be our God.
We are your people.   M. L.

How confidently and prayerfully
do I turn to Jesus in time of need?

They stand best who kneel most.
E. C. McKenzie

Parables are mirrors

A scene in *Hamlet* has the young prince confront his mother, the queen, saying:

*"Come and sit down. You shall not budge . . .
till I set you up a glass
Where you may see the inmost part of you."
[His mother cries,]
"O Hamlet, speak no more.
Thou turn'st my eyes into my very soul.
And there I see such black and grained spots."*

What Hamlet asked his mother to look into was not a glass mirror. He asked her to look into her own soul and see her ugly part in his father's tragic murder.

This brings us to Jesus' parables.
Jesus composed many of them in such a way that the people in his parables "mirrored" people in his listening audience.

For example, his parable of the sower describes four kinds of soil into which seed falls: hard, thorn-covered, rocky, good. These soils mirror the four kinds of hearts into which God's word falls.
Yves Congar writes:

*The parables, then,
are like a collection of mirrors
in which I am invited to see myself. . . .
Is it not I who received the seed
of God's Word as though on rocks?
I who let it be choked by thorns? . . .
When I ask myself questions like this,
the parables reveal me to myself.*
Jesus Christ

This week's meditations focus on Jesus' parables.
We reflect on how Jesus used them as "mirrors" in which his audience could see their hearts as they really were—open or closed to God's word.

Suggested daily readings

1 Jesus used parables to teach   Mt 13:34–35

2 Parable of the sower   Mt 13:1–9

3 Parable of the sower explained   Mt 13:18–23

4 Parable of two sons   Mt 21:28–32

5 Parable of Lazarus   Lk 16:19–31

6 Parable of the Good Samaritan   Lk 10:25–37

7 Parable of the children at play   Mt 11:16–19

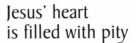

Jesus uses parables
to teach us

Journal

*Jesus used parables to tell all these things
to the crowds.*   Matthew 13:34

One day a fish came upon divers
photographing the dark depths of the ocean.
He swam off to warn the fish elders
about the weird invaders from outerwater.
But the elders ridiculed him, saying,
"There's no life in outerwater—
too much oxygen and far too little water.
Besides, the bright sun would kill all life."
Someone used this modern "parable"
to illustrate how hard it is
to explain to people anything
that is beyond their everyday experience.
Jesus had a similar problem when he tried
to explain God's Kingdom to people.
It was too far beyond their experience.
And so he turned to parables.

Why were parables useful in helping people
grasp truths beyond their experience?
What is one such truth I find hard to grasp?

*Parables are
earthly stories with heavenly meanings.
They build a bridge
from the known to the unknown.
They prod the imagination and stretch the mind
to embrace spiritual realities
beyond our ordinary, earthly experience.*

Journal

Jesus tells us
the parable of the sower

[Jesus said, "A farmer planted seed.
Some fell on the path and birds ate it.
Some fell on rocky soil, grew quickly,
but died when the sun baked the soil.]
Some of the seed fell among thorn bushes,
which grew up and choked the plants.
But some seeds fell in good soil."   Matthew 13:7–8

A teacher explained that the seed
stood for God's word, and the seedbeds
stood for the four kinds of hearts
into which God's word can fall.
Then she asked her students to write down
(1) what seedbed their own heart is like,
(2) why it is like this, and
(3) how they might change their situation.
One boy wrote:
"My heart is most like the thorn bushes.
I hear God's word in church,
but I forget it as soon as I return home.
This is because my father is mentally sick,
which puts my family on edge. I don't know
what I can do to change my situation."

How would I respond to the boy?
What seedbed is my heart most like?
Why? How might I improve my situation?

[The Lord told Paul in prayer,] "My grace
is all you need, for my power is greatest
when you are weak."   2 Corinthians 12:9

Jesus explains to us
the parable of the sower

[Jesus said in the parable of the sower,]
"The seeds that fell among thorn bushes
stand for those who hear the message;
but the worries about this life
and the love for riches choke the message,
and they don't bear fruit."　Matthew 13:22

In his youth the French novelist
Honoré de Balzac was practically starving
and living in a one-room apartment.
One night a thief entered and
was trying to pick the lock on his desk.
Suddenly, a loud laugh totally shattered
the thief's composure. It came from Balzac.
He had been in bed, watching the thief work.
When the thief recovered from shock,
he asked, "Why do you laugh?" Balzac said,
"I'm laughing at the risk you're taking
to try to find money in my desk by night,
when I can't find any in it by day."

To what extent is worrying about money—
or other things—choking God's word in me?
What might Jesus be saying to me?

I refuse to worry about the future.
When I was a little kid, one of the
surprising things my father told me—
and it has really worked for me—
was that it was a sin to worry too much.
　　　　　　　　　　　　　　Actor Mel Gibson

Journal

Jesus tells us
the parable of the two sons

[Jesus told a parable about a father.
He said to his son,]
"'Go and work in the vineyard today.'
'I don't want to,' he answered,
but later he changed his mind and went."

Matthew 21:28–29

The film *Tom Brown's School Days*
concerns a popular boy who lived with
about a dozen other boys in the dormitory
of a British boarding school.
One night a new boy innocently knelt
beside his bed to say his prayers.
Several older boys poked fun at him.
That night Tom lay awake thinking about
what had happened. He also thought about
how his mother taught him to pray nightly—
something he no longer did.
The next night several boys were planning
to poke more fun at the new boy.
When bedtime came, however, something
unexpected happened to change their plans.
When the new boy knelt down
to say his prayers, so did Tom.

How does Jesus' parable of the two sons
act as a mirror parable? What is one thing
in my life that I should change?

When you're through changing,
you're through.   Bruce Barton

Jesus tells us the parable
of a poor man and a rich man

Journal

[Jesus told a parable about a rich man
who was in Hades for grossly ignoring
the sad plight of a poor man.
The poor man, whose name was Lazarus,]
"used to be brought to the rich man's door,
hoping to eat the bits of food that fell
from the rich man's table."   Luke 16:20–21

This parable inspired the stirring homily of
Pope John Paul II at Yankee Stadium in 1979.
He said, "We cannot stand idly by, enjoying
our own riches and freedom if, in any place,
the Lazarus of the 20th century stands
at our doors. . . . The rich man and Lazarus
are both human beings,
both of them equally created
in the image and likeness of God,
both of them equally redeemed by Christ."

How does the parable of Lazarus and the
rich man act as a mirror to me? How might
I respond to what I see in the mirror?

The poor
of the United States and of the world
are your brothers and sisters in Christ.
You must never be content
to leave them just the crumbs of the feast.
You must give of your substance,
and not just of your abundance.
                              Yankee Stadium homily

Jesus tells us the parable of the Good Samaritan

[Jesus told a parable about] "a man who was going down from Jerusalem to Jericho when robbers attacked him . . . leaving him half dead. . . . When a priest saw the man, he walked on by. . . . A Samaritan . . . saw him . . . and took him to an inn, where he took care of him." Luke 10:30–31, 33–34

Saint John Chrysostom was a bishop who lived about 300 years after Jesus. In a provocative homily, he said of people who wanted to adorn the church with gold: "Of what use is it to weigh down Christ's table with golden cups . . . but not give a cup of water [to the needy]? What is the use of providing the table with cloths woven of gold thread, and not providing Christ himself with the clothes he needs? . . . I am not forbidding you to supply these ornaments; I am urging you to provide these other things as well, and indeed to provide them first. . . . Do not, therefore, adorn the church and ignore your afflicted brother, for he is the most precious temple of all."

Am I more like the priest or the Samaritan?

No greater burden can be borne . . . than to know that no one cares about or understands [my plight]. Arthur H. Stanback

Journal

Jesus tells us the parable of the children at play

*Jesus said, "Now, to what can I compare
the people of this day? They are like children
sitting in the marketplace.
One group shouts to the other,
'We played wedding music for you, but
you wouldn't dance! We sang funeral songs,
but you wouldn't cry!' When John came,
he fasted and drank no wine,
and everyone said, 'He has a demon in him!'
When the Son of Man came, he ate and drank,
and everyone said, 'Look at this man! He is
a glutton and wine drinker.' "* Matthew 11:16–19

The *Christian Science Monitor*
received this letter:
"When I subscribed a year ago, you stated
that if I was not satisfied at the end
of the year I could have my money back.
Well, I would like my money back.
On second thought,
to save you the trouble, you may apply it
to my next year's subscription."

When I meet people like the children in Jesus'
parable and like the subscriber to the paper,
how do I usually react? To what extent
do the children in the parable mirror me?

*People are unreasonable,
illogical and self-centered.
Love them anyway!* Theodore Roethke

Parables are windows

The movie *The Heart Is a Lonely Hunter*
has a teenage girl trying to explain
to a deaf-mute what music is like.
She stands in front of him and gestures
with her hands and face. But to no avail.
Finally, they both give up and laugh.

Jesus faced a similar challenge
when he tried to explain to people
what the Kingdom of God was like.
It was something beyond their experience.
At best, Jesus could give them
only a vague idea of what it was like.

And so he constructed some of his parables
to act as "windows"
through which people could "look"
and get a better understanding
of God's Kingdom. Thus, Jesus said:

"What shall we say
the Kingdom of God is like? . . .
What parable shall we use to explain it?
It is like this. A man takes a mustard seed,
the smallest seed in the world,
and plants it in the ground.
After a while it grows up
and becomes the biggest of all plants.
It puts out such large branches
that the birds come and make their nests
in its shade."   Mark 4:30–32

Jesus' point is this:
God's Kingdom might seem tiny now,
but it will grow great in size
and spread to every nation on earth.

And so besides functioning as *mirrors,*
some of Jesus' parables function, also,
as *windows* through which people can look
and get a faint glimpse of what Jesus means
when he talks about God's Kingdom.

This week's meditations focus on
seven of Jesus' window parables
and how God can still use them
to speak to us in our personal lives.

Suggested daily readings

1 Parable of the treasure   Mt 13:44
2 Parable of the workers   Mt 20:1–16
3 Parable of the growing seed   Mk 4:26–29
4 Parable of the vineyard owner   Mt 21:33–46
5 Parable of the mustard seed   Mt 13:31–32
6 Parable of the talents   Mt 25:14–30
7 Parable of the pearl buyer   Mt 13:45–46

Jesus tells us the parable of the buried treasure

Journal

Jesus said,
"The Kingdom of heaven is like this.
A man happens to find a treasure hidden
in a field. He . . . sells everything he has . . .
and buys that field." Matthew 13:44

Abraham Lincoln was a great storyteller.
Explaining why he told stories, he said:
"It is not the story itself,
but its purpose, or effect, that interests me.
I often avoid a long and useless discussion . . .
by telling a short story."
Jesus told stories for the same reason.
For example, when someone asked Jesus,
"Who is my neighbor?" Jesus avoided a long
discussion by telling the story
of the Good Samaritan. Luke 10:25–37
Lincoln also said of stories, "The edge
of a rebuke may be blunted by a story."
Jesus did this also. For example, he blunted
the edge of a rebuke of Simon the Pharisee
by telling a story. Luke 7:36–50

Robert Frost once said,
"Society can never think things out.
It has to see them acted out by actors."
How do stories do this?

I am always ready to learn,
although I do not always like being taught.
Winston Churchill

Jesus tells us the parable of the vineyard workers

Jesus said, "The Kingdom of heaven is like this. [A man went out five times in one day to hire workers. At day's end, he paid them all a full day's wage. When the first workers complained, he said,] 'Are you jealous because I am generous?'" Matthew 20:1, 15

One day Henry heard glass breaking. Running outside with a portable phone, he saw two boys next to the house throwing stones at bottles. Seeing Henry on the phone, they thought he was calling the police and started throwing stones at him. He dropped the phone and cornered the boys. To their surprise, he told them, "I was planning to clean up the lot anyway, and I'll pay you five dollars each to help me." They saw he was serious and jumped at it. An hour later two more boys joined them. When they finished, Henry paid each boy five dollars.To Henry's surprise, the first two boys complained that this wasn't fair. Henry said later, "It was a repeat of the gospel story; people haven't changed in 2,000 years."

How might the point of Jesus' parable apply to me in my life, right now?

The only person worth envying is the person who doesn't envy. E. C. McKenzie

Journal

Jesus tells us the parable of the yeast

Jesus told them still another parable:
"The Kingdom of heaven is like this.
A woman takes some yeast and mixes it
with a bushel of flour until
the whole batch of dough rises."   Matthew 13:33

A teacher told her class, "When I was a girl,
my grandma gave me a big cucumber
inside a bottle with a narrow neck.
She said she'd tell me a 'big secret' when
I figured out how she got it into the bottle.
One day I was walking in Grandma's garden,
and I saw a bottle into which she had
inserted a vine with a tiny cucumber on it.
Now I knew how she got the cucumber
in the bottle; she grew it there.
Then Grandma told me her 'big secret.'
She said a 'good habit' formed in childhood
is like a tiny cucumber inserted in a bottle—
or like a tiny bit of yeast inserted in dough.
The habit grows so big and strong inside you
that no one can take it away from you."

What is one good habit,
formed in childhood,
that has grown bigger in me? What is
one bad habit that I regret forming?

First we form habits, then they form us.
Conquer your bad habits, or they'll
eventually conquer you.   Dr. Rob Gilbert

59

Journal

Jesus tells us the parable of the fig tree

*[Jesus told a parable about a man
who told his gardener to cut down a tree
because it failed to produce any figs.]
"But the gardener answered, 'Leave it alone,
sir, just one more year; I will dig around it
and put in some fertilizer.
Then if the tree bears figs next year,
so much the better; if not,
then you can have it cut down.' "* Luke 13:8–9

In *Uncommon Friends,* James Newton says
Thomas Edison and a team of assistants
had just finished making improvements
on the first lightbulb. Edison gave the bulb
"to a young helper, who nervously
carried it upstairs, step by step.
At the last moment, the boy dropped it.
The whole team had to work
another 24 hours to make another bulb.
Edison looked around,
then handed it to the same boy.
The gesture probably changed the boy's life.
Edison knew
that more than the bulb was at stake."

In what sense is Newton's story of Edison
an application of Jesus' parable? What
might Jesus be saying to me through it?

*Sympathy is two hearts
tugging at the same load.* E. C. McKenzie

Jesus tells us the parable
of the mustard seed

Journal

Jesus asked,
"What is the Kingdom of God like?
What shall I compare it with?
It is like this. A man takes
a mustard seed and plants it in his field.
The plant grows and becomes a tree."

Luke 13:18–19

In 1990, Secretary of State James Baker
convened the Arab-Israeli peace talks
in Madrid, saying,
"The road to peace is very long
and it is very difficult.
We have to crawl before we can walk
and we have to walk before we run,
and today I think we all began to crawl."
What Baker said about the road to peace
can be said about so many things in life:
success, holiness, happiness.
The road to them is long and difficult.
And the first step is always a "crawl."
But if we begin and persevere,
this mustard-seed beginning
will someday grow into a great tree.

At what stage am I on the road to my dream:
crawling, walking, or running?

The future belongs to those
who believe in the beauty of their dreams.

Eleanor Roosevelt

Journal

Jesus tells us the parable of the talents

[Jesus told a parable about a man who summoned his servants and gave each of them a sum of money, saying,]
" 'See what you can earn with this.' " Luke 19:13

A famous violin maker
said the best wood for violins
comes from the north side of the tree.
The reason is that it has been seasoned
by the cold north wind.
And that seasoning gives it a special sound.
The same is true of human beings.
Some of the world's greatest people
have been seasoned by suffering.
Take Beethoven. The son of an alcoholic
father, he lost his hearing at 28.
When he conducted the first performance
of his Ninth Symphony, he couldn't hear
the music, except in his mind.
Nor could he hear the thunderous applause
that followed the performance.

People complain that some handicap or
obstacle keeps them from "earning more"
with the talent ("gold coin") God gave them.
How might just the opposite be true?

The "gold coins" God gives me
often include some handicap or situation
that can make me either bitter or better.
And I am the one who decides.

Jesus tells us the parable of the pearl buyer

*[Jesus compared God's Kingdom
to a man in search of fine pearls.]
"When he finds one that is unusually fine,
he goes and sells everything he has,
and buys that pearl."* Matthew 13:46

Johnny Unitas was someone
in search of a dream: playing football.
But the colleges told him he was too small.
He kept searching; finally, a small college
gave him a chance. He excelled.
After college, he kept searching, but in vain.
He got a job, and played weekend ball
at six dollars a game to perfect his skill.
In a surprise break, he tried out
with the Baltimore Colts and was signed.
When quarterback George Shaw was injured,
Johnny Unitas got his chance.
The rest is history. He became a great star
and was voted into the pro Hall of Fame.

Jesus invites me to pursue God's Kingdom
as did the pearl buyer in the Gospel
and as did the dreamer, Johnny Unitas.
He promises, not fame that will pass,
but eternal happiness that will never end.
How am I responding to Jesus' invitation?

*The bitterest tears shed over graves
are for words left unsaid and
deeds left undone.* Harriet Beecher Stowe

What is the Kingdom like?

The miracles of Jesus
exploded across the night sky
like thunderclaps and lightning bolts.
They heralded
the arrival of something spectacular.

Like cosmic alarm clocks,
they awakened a sleeping world
to the dawn of a new era:
the Kingdom of God.

By his miracles
Jesus shattered the walls of indifference,
crumbled the walls of unconcern,
and announced the victory
of light over darkness, good over evil,
and life over death.

The rallying call,
"Thy Kingdom come!"
was to ring out and ring out.
Jesus told people
to tattoo it on their hearts,
to sing it around night campfires, and
to proclaim it from the housetops.
But most of all, Jesus told people
to do something about it, saying:

"You are like light
for the whole world. . . .
Your light must shine before people,

so that they will see the good things you do
and praise your Father in heaven."
Matthew 5:14, 16

Last week's meditations centered on how
Jesus used parables to introduce people to
the revolutionary nature of God's Kingdom.
This week's meditations focus on
Jesus' description of God's Kingdom.

Prayer procedure

You might say the Lord's Prayer
at the end of each meditation
in a slightly audible voice,
stressing the petition "thy Kingdom come."

Suggested daily readings

1 Coming of the Kingdom   Lk 17:20–30
2 Membership in the Kingdom   Mt 7:21–23
3 The poor and the Kingdom   Mt 5:1–12
4 The rich young man   Mt 19:16–22
5 The rich and the Kingdom   Mt 19:23–30
6 Parable of the two builders   Mt 7:24–27
7 Great and least in the Kingdom Mt 5:17–20

Jesus says, "God's Kingdom is within you"

Jesus said,
"The Kingdom of God does not come
in such a way as to be seen.
No one will say, 'Look, here it is!' or,
'There it is!'; because the Kingdom of God
is within you."　Luke 17:20–21

An old man lived in an old shack at the end
of the Street of the Lost Angel
in Krakow, Poland.
One night he dreamed about a treasure
hidden in an old shack under a bridge
in Warsaw. The dream was so real
that he went to Warsaw.
When he found the shack under the bridge,
a homeless youth was living in it.
The man told the youth about his dream,
planning to share the treasure with him.
"That's really weird!" said the youth.
"Last night I dreamed about a treasure hidden
in the shack of an old man
on the Street of the Lost Angel in Krakow.
My dream was so real that I planned
to journey to Krakow to find the treasure."

What is the point of this old story?
What is the treasure of my dreams?
Where has my search for it taken me?

The greatest treasure isn't far, far away;
it is closer to me than my own breath.

Journal

_____

_____

_____

_____

_____

_____

_____

_____

_____

Journal

_____

_____

_____

_____

_____

_____

_____

_____

_____

_____

Jesus says, "Not everyone will enter God's Kingdom"

Jesus said, "Not everyone who calls me 'Lord, Lord' will enter the Kingdom of heaven, but only those who do what my Father . . . wants them to do." Matthew 7:21

In *American Way* magazine a cartoon
by W. B. Park shows a man in his fifties
dressed in a baseball suit and hat.
He is seated in an easy chair.
Resting against one side of the chair
are a baseball bat and glove.
On the other side of the chair is a table
with a telephone on it.
Across from the man sits his wife.
She wears a patient but frustrated look.
The caption reads:
"I don't want to step on your dream, Walter,
but if they haven't called after thirty years,
perhaps it's time to go on to something else."
That cartoon makes a good point.
There's a time to dream,
but there's also a time to face up to reality
and assume responsibility for your life.
The same is true of God's Kingdom.

In what area of my life might I be failing
to assume responsibility for my life
and do what God wants me to do?

*You can't steal second base
and keep your foot on first.* Frederick R. Wilcox

Jesus says, "God's Kingdom belongs to the poor in spirit"

Journal

*Jesus said, "Happy are those
who know they are spiritually poor;
the Kingdom of heaven belongs to them!"*
                                    Matthew 5:3

At age 40, Lee Atwater was known
for his savvy, vitality, and charisma.
He was President Bush's campaign manager
and had a bright future ahead of him.
Then his health suddenly went bad.
The problem turned out to be a brain tumor
that would take his life quickly.
During his illness, he observed
that something was not right,
both with our society and himself.
Then he noted:
"My illness helped me to see
that what was missing in society
is what is missing in me—
a little heart, a lot of brotherhood."
He concluded, "We must . . . speak
to this spiritual vacuum
at the heart of American society."

What can just one person do
when it comes to speaking to the
spiritual vacuum in American society?

*Who loseth wealth loseth much . . .
but who loseth the spirit loseth all.*
                Elbert Hubbard (slightly adapted)

Jesus says, "Many who now are first will be last"

Jesus said,
"It will be very hard for rich people
to enter the Kingdom of heaven. . . .
Many who now are first will be last."
Matthew 19:23, 30

"Column 8" is an extremely popular daily
newspaper column in Australia.
It features human interest stories.
For example, one story concerns a man
in economy class on a plane. He objects
to sitting next to a woman of color.
Since the economy class section is full,
the man demands that the flight attendant
check to see if there is an open seat
in the business-class section.
The flight attendant comes back smiling.
As the man begins to unbuckle his seat belt
to prepare to move to the more expensive
section of the plane, the flight attendant
says to the woman of color,
"Madam, please follow me and I'll take you
to the business section."

Why would/wouldn't this be something
that Jesus might have done
had he been the flight attendant?

Creating all people free and equal
isn't enough. Some means must be devised
to keep them free and equal.   E. C. McKenzie

Journal

Jesus says, "Entering God's Kingdom is not easy"

Jesus said,
"It is much harder for a rich person
to enter the Kingdom of God
than for a camel to go through
the eye of a needle."   Mark 10:25

Fishing boats made Monterey, California,
a "pelican's paradise."
Fishermen cleaned their fish
and threw the entrails to the waiting birds.
It was all play and no worry for pelicans.
The good life was theirs to milk and enjoy.
Then something terrible happened.
Entrails became commercially valuable.
Overnight, the pelicans lost their "good life."
Worse yet, the "good life" had made them
so content and soft that they had lost
not only the art of survival but also
the discipline for survival. The result?
Vast segments of the pelican population
grew weak and died of starvation.

How might the pelican story serve as a
commentary on why it might be so hard
for the rich to enter God's Kingdom?

Who never ate bread in sorrow,
Who never spent the darksome hours
Weeping and watching for the morrow
He knows you not, you heavenly Powers.
            Johann Wolfgang von Goethe

Journal

Journal

_____

_____

_____

_____

_____

_____

_____

_____

_____

_____

Jesus explains who will be great in God's Kingdom

*Jesus said, "Whoever obeys the Law
and teaches others to do the same,
will be great in the Kingdom of heaven."*
Matthew 5:19

Author Jerome Weidman attended
a public school on New York's East Side.
He had a third grade math teacher
named Mrs. O'Neill.
One day when she was grading test papers,
she noticed that 18 students had given
the same odd wrong answer to a question.
The next day she asked the 12 students
to stay after the dismissal bell.
Then without accusing any of them,
she wrote 18 words on the chalkboard:
"The measure of our real character is what
we would do if we would never be found out."
She then added the name of the person
who said them: Thomas Babington Macaulay.
Weidman said later: "I don't know about
the other 11 students. Speaking for only one
of the dozen with whom I am on intimate
terms, I can say this: it was the most
important single lesson of my life."

Can I recall an important lesson
that someone taught me in my youth?

*Don't compromise yourself.
You are all you've got.*   Janis Joplin

Jesus says, "To enter God's Kingdom, do God's will"

Jesus said,
"Anyone who hears these words of mine
and does not obey them
is like a foolish man
who built his house on sand.
The rain poured down,
the rivers flooded over,
the wind blew hard against that house,
and it fell. And what a terrible fall
that was!"   Matthew 7:26–27

In his book *The Great Divorce,*
the British theologian C. S. Lewis
divides the world into two groups of people,
those who say to God,
'Thy will be done,'
and those to whom God says,
'All right, then, have it your way.' "

Lewis's division of the world
invites me to reflect on the question,
Into which of the two groups
do I most often find myself?
What is one area
in which I find God's will hard to accept?

I just want to do God's will. . . .
I'm happy tonight. . . .
I'm not fearing any man.
Martin Luther King Jr. in a speech on April 3, 1968,
the eve of his assassination

Who is Jesus?

Avery Dulles wrote a milestone book
called *Apologetics and the Biblical Christ.*
One statement in the book surprised
a lot of people. Dulles wrote:

*Jesus constantly does
the most unexpected things, revolutionizing
the accepted norms of conduct.
He praises pagans and prostitutes,
draws near to Samaritans and lepers.*

*He attacks the most respected classes,
and insults his hosts at dinner. . . .
He finds time to welcome little children. . . .
He rebukes the wind and the waves,
and falls silent before his accusers. . . .*

*Men would never have fabricated
such a . . . religious leader,
and precisely for this reason
the Gospels have undying power
to convert humble hearts.*

British theologian C. S. Lewis
takes Dulles's point a step further, saying:

*[A man] who said
the sort of things Jesus said . . .
would either be a lunatic or the Devil. . . .
You must make your choice.
Either this man was, and is,
the Son of God*

*or else a madman or something worse.
You can . . . kill him as a demon,
or you can fall at his feet
and call him Lord and God.*

*But let us not
come with any patronizing nonsense
about his being a great human teacher.
He has not left that open to us.
He did not intend to.*

This week's meditations focus on answers
to that awesome question of questions:
Who is Jesus?

Suggested daily readings

1	Lamb of God	Jn 1:19–31
2	Son of God	Jn 1:32–34
3	Messiah of Israel	Jn 1:35–42
4	Son of Man	Jn 1:43–50
5	Good Shepherd	Jn 10:1–16
6	Light of the World	Jn 8:12–18
7	Resurrection and the Life	Jn 11:17–27

Jesus is
the "Lamb of God"

John the Baptist saw Jesus coming . . .
and said, "There is the Lamb of God,
who takes away the sin of the world!
This is the one I was talking about."
John 1:29–30

Describing his life in postwar Germany,
Bruce Larson says, "I felt
that I was swimming in a sea of garbage.
Worse yet, the garbage was inside me."
Then one night Bruce was standing guard
in a bombed-out building in Stuttgart.
As he lifted his eyes skyward,
he could see millions of stars
shining through the charred rafters
of the wrecked building.
With all the faith he could muster,
he prayed, "Lord, if you are really there,
and if you really care, take over my life."
That night, Bruce Larson met Jesus Christ
and understood for the very first time
what John the Baptist meant when he said,
"There is the Lamb of God,
who takes away the sin of the world!"

What moment in my life comes closest
to paralleling this moment
in Larson's life?

"To understand,
you must turn from evil."   Job 28:28

Journal

Journal

_____

_____

_____

_____

_____

_____

_____

_____

_____

_____

_____

Jesus is the "Son of God"

John gave this testimony:
"I saw the Spirit come down like a dove
from heaven and stay on him. . . .
I tell you that he is the Son of God."
John 1:32, 34

Paul Waldemann came from a Jewish family.
One day a "startling question" popped into
his mind: Could Jesus really be God?
He tried to dismiss the thought,
but it kept returning to him.
And so he began to read up on the matter.
But reading only confused him more.
Finally, he asked a priest—a former Jew—
to help him reach clarity. The priest said,
"Speak to God in your own words.
Ask him to lead you." Waldemann writes:
"For weeks on end . . . I pleaded with God,
'Please show me what you want me to do.
I want to do your will.'
But he remained silent. . . .
[Then one evening God answered my prayer.]
I was filled with a peace . . .
I had never known before."
Richer Than a Millionaire: One Man's Journey to God

What is the link between study and prayer,
and how do I decide when to do what?

When Jesus teaches me to sing his song,
how can I keep from singing it? Author unknown

Jesus is
the "Messiah of Israel"

[One day Jesus asked his disciples,]
"Who do you say I am?"
Simon Peter answered,
"You are the Messiah."   Matthew 16:15–16

An old story concerns an innocent fugitive
fleeing hostile government soldiers.
Some friendly villagers fed and hid him.
The next morning the soldiers showed up and
threatened to destroy the village by noon
if the fugitive's hideout was not revealed.
Some villagers went to the old rabbi's cave
outside the town to seek his advice.
The old man opened his Bible for an answer.
His eyes fell on the words, "It is better
for one man to die than for all to perish."
He told the villagers to hand over the man.
Later an angel appeared to the rabbi
and said, "What have you done?
That young man was the Messiah!"
The rabbi wept, saying, "How was I to know?"
The angel said, "You should've met with him
and looked into his eyes.
Then you would have known."

To know that Jesus is the Messiah
I must meet with him personally
and look into his eyes. How do I do this?

Turn to the Lord and pray to him,
now that he is near.   Isaiah 55:6

Journal

Jesus is
the "Son of Man"

Jesus said,
"The Son of man . . . [came] to give his life
to redeem many people."   Matthew 20:28

Little Jason was returning home
later and later each afternoon from school.
His father lectured him on punctuality,
but it made little impact on the boy.
Finally, he told Jason,
"The next time you come home late,
you can expect bread and water for supper."
Sure enough, the next night Jason was late.
When he sat down to supper,
he was stunned.
On his plate was a single slice of bread.
Jason saw that his father meant business.
When the punishment had sunk in fully,
Jason's father gave him his own full plate
and took Jason's single slice of bread.
That was all Jason's father ate that night.
Years later, Jason said that what his father
did at supper that night taught him
in the most eloquent way what Jesus did
for the human race 2,000 years ago.

What did Jesus do for us 2,000 years ago?
What am I doing in return for Jesus today?

"[The LORD's servant] endured
the suffering that should have been ours,
the pain that we should have borne."   Isaiah 53:4

Jesus is
the "Light of the World"

Jesus said, "I am the light of the world.
Whoever follows me will have the light of
life and will never walk in darkness."   John 8:12

Country music singer Hank Williams
wrote a song called "I Saw the Light."
It's about a person stumbling in the night,
refusing to let the Savior in.
Suddenly a stranger appears: Jesus.
At once the song shifts
from sadness to gladness
and goes something like this:
"Praise Jesus; I saw the light.
No more stumbling in the night!
No more groping in the dark.
Praise Jesus; I saw the light."
Every one of us
can relate to Hank Williams's song.
We have all foundered in the night,
refusing to let the Savior in.
Then Jesus appeared.
"Praise the Lord; we saw the light."

To what extent am I still stumbling
in the night, refusing to let the Savior in?

From all that dwell below the skies
Let the Creator's praise arise:
Let the Redeemer's name be sung
Through every land, by every tongue.
                              Isaac Watts (1715)

Journal

_____
_____
_____
_____
_____
_____
_____
_____
_____

Jesus is
the "Good Shepherd"

Jesus said, "I am the good shepherd.
As the Father knows me and
I know the Father,
in the same way I know my sheep
and they know me."   John 10:14–15

In ancient England, dinner guests used to
entertain other guests after meals.
At one dinner an actor was present
and did a fabulous rendition of Psalm 23,
"The Lord is my shepherd."
Everyone stood and applauded.
Then a guest noticed the aunt of the host
dozing in the back of the room.
The old woman was deaf and had missed
almost all of the entertainment.
The guest shouted, "Auntie, come up and
do something." Everyone applauded.
She recited the same psalm.
When she finished, there wasn't a dry eye
in the room. Later, the guest asked the actor,
"Your rendition was fabulous.
So why were we so moved by the aunt?"
He replied, "Simple—I know the psalm,
but old auntie knows the shepherd."

How well do I know the shepherd?

In prayer it is better
to have a heart without words
than words without a heart.   John Bunyan

Jesus is the "Resurrection and the Life"

Jesus said,
"I am the resurrection and the life.
Those who believe in me will live." John 11:25

Robert McAfee Brown was on a troop ship
bringing marines back from Japan.
One day they were studying the raising
of Lazarus. After the session a marine said,
"God seemed to speak to me today."
He went on to explain that while in Japan,
he did something that filled him with guilt.
He had even considered suicide.
During the session, the thought struck him
that since Jesus was a man like him,
he could understand his situation.
And since Jesus was also God, he could help
him in the most powerful way imaginable.
He could raise him to new life,
as he did Lazarus. In short, the marine
had discovered in a personal way
that Jesus was indeed "the resurrection
and the life"—not only in the life to come
but also in this life right now.

How do I want Jesus to be my resurrection
and my life in this life right now?

The Easter Message means
that God can turn . . . broken reeds
like Simon Peter into rocks.
Fulton Sheen

Pray as Jesus did

Joseph Chilton Pearce did research work
on child development. One research project
involved "happy, brilliant" children
and what "commonality" they shared.

The result was startling—"not because
it yielded only one commonality, but because
of the nature of the commonality."
The thing that "tied them together in their
early age" was "they spent vast amounts
of time in open-eyed, blank staring."

"The children," explained Pearce, "were
engaging in a natural kind of meditation"
that greatly enhanced their ability to learn.
When these kids engaged in blank staring,
"they pulled out their sensory plugs,"
allowing them to "exclude the world
and escape into themselves."
During this time, they balanced
what was going on outside and inside.

Ultimately, says Pearce,
this "balancing" is what learning is about.
And it is this "balance" that brings about
a remarkable contentment and happiness.

Something similar happens in prayer.
We escape into ourselves for a time to balance
what is going on outside and inside.
Jesus did this often.

At every operative event
in his life we find him at prayer.
He prayed at his baptism (Luke 3:21),
before preaching and healing (Mark 1:35),
after preaching and healing (Luke 5:16),
before picking his disciples (Luke 6:12),
before instructing his disciples (Luke 9:18),
before teaching them to pray (Luke 11:1),
before going to Jerusalem (Luke 9:29),
at the Last Supper (John 17:1–26),
at Gethsemane (Luke 22:41),
on the cross (Luke 23:34).

This week's meditations focus on the value
and importance of praying as Jesus prayed.

Suggested daily readings

1 Jesus prays in early morning		Mk 1:35–39
2 Jesus prays in small groups		Lk 9:28–36
3 Jesus prays in community		Lk 4:16–21
4 Jesus prays in private		Mt 6:5–6
5 Jesus prays "Our Father"		Mt 6:7–15
6 Jesus prays humbly		Lk 18:9–14
7 Jesus prays confidently		Lk 18:1–8

Jesus goes off
to a lonely place to pray

Long before daylight, Jesus got up and . . .
went out of town to a lonely place,
where he prayed. Mark 1:35

When winter comes to the South Pole,
total darkness sets in. Richard Byrd braved
four and a half months of this darkness
gathering weather data—alone. Why alone?
He answers,
"To taste peace, quiet, and solitude. . . .
It was all that simple. . . .
We are caught up in the winds that blow
every which way. . . . The thinking man
is driven . . . to long desperately
for some quiet place where he can reason
undisturbed and take inventory." *Alone*
The South Pole experience changed Byrd
dramatically. He writes: "I live
more simply now and with more peace."
Jesus spent a prolonged period in prayer
at the start of his ministry.
And during his ministry, he continued
to set aside times when he would go off alone
to pray undisturbed.

What is one change that I have noticed
in my life since I began my "prayer journey"?

When we begin to live more seriously inside,
we begin to live more simply outside.
Ernest Hemingway

Journal

Jesus departs by boat by himself

*When Jesus heard the news about
[the beheading of John the Baptist] . . .
he left there in a boat and went
to a lonely place by himself.*   Matthew 14:13

Author Anne Morrow Lindbergh loved
walking along a deserted beach all alone.
The rhythmic sound of the waves,
the soothing sun on her bare back,
and the mist from sea spray in her hair
gave her a feeling of peace and well-being.
She enjoyed, especially, walking into the surf
and out again, like a sandpiper.
In her book *Gifts from the Sea,* she writes:
"These are among the most important times
in one's life—when one is alone.
The artist knows he must be alone to create;
the writer, to work out his thoughts;
the musician, to compose; the saint to pray."

If I cannot go off to a beach to be alone
and meditate, what are my alternatives?

*Because I am a woman involved
in practical cares, I . . . must meditate
when I can, early in the morning and
on the fly during the day. Not in the privacy
of a study—but here, there and everywhere—
at the kitchen table . . .
on my way to and from appointments.*
Dorothy Day, *House of Hospitality*

Jesus says,
"Close the door and pray"

Journal

Jesus said, "When you pray,
go to your room, close the door,
and pray to your Father, who is unseen.
And your Father, who sees what you do
in private, will reward you."   Matthew 6:6

Rabbi David Wolpe authored the book
Teaching Your Child about God.
In it, he tells a story about a rabbi's child,
who began wandering into a nearby woods.
This concerned the rabbi because
the woods were dark and dangerous.
So one day he said to the child,
"I have noticed that each afternoon
you wander off into the woods.
What do you do in such a dangerous place?"
The child said, "I go there to find God."
"That is a good thing; I'm glad that
you are searching for God," said the father.
"But, my child, don't you know
that God is the same everywhere?"
"Yes," the boy answered, "but I'm not."

What is the point of Rabbi Wolpe's story?
Where do I find God most easily?

Oh, help me, Lord, to take the time
To set all else aside,
That in the secret place of prayer
I may with Thee abide.
                    Author unknown

Journal

Jesus is asked,
"Lord, teach us to pray"

One day Jesus was praying. . . .
When he had finished,
one of his disciples said to him,
"Lord, teach us to pray."   Luke 11:1

A man named Spriggs recalls
his first night as a homeless person.
Someone directed him to a shelter.
There he found a lot of rough-looking men
waiting in line.
Finally, the door opened and they all got beds—
about a hundred men in all.
Minutes later, they turned out the lights.
Spriggs writes: "I was terrified. . . .
Then out of the darkness a voice said,
'Our Father, who are in heaven . . .'
and the entire dormitory joined in.
At the end of the prayer another voice began,
'Now I lay me down to sleep . . .'
Even now I get goosebumps
thinking about it.
That minute I realized that God . . .
seems to be closer to the homeless.
You could feel him in the shelter. . . .
My fears were replaced by peace."
The Catholic Standard, Washington, D.C.

Can I recall ever feeling God's presence—
perhaps when I was alone and frightened?

Go to sleep in peace. God is awake.   Victor Hugo

Jesus explains how we should pray

Jesus said,
"This, then, is how you should pray:
'Our Father in heaven.'"   Matthew 6:9

In his book *God Calling,* A. J. Russell
has God ask the reader this question:
"Have you ever thought what it means
to be able to summon at will
the God of the World?"
God goes on to say that even important people
cannot visit a head of state
with such freedom of access.
They must make an appointment
well in advance. Then God says:
"But to my subjects I have given the right
to enter My Presence when they will.
Nay more, they can summon Me
to bedside, to workshop—and I am there.
Could Divine Love do more?"

How deeply do I appreciate being able
to summon God to my side, wherever I am,
at any time of the day or night
without having to make an appointment?

Before the judgment seat
one of the most embarrassing things
that we will have to answer for
will be our lack of prayer—
one of God's greatest gifts to us.
                              Anonymous

Journal

Jesus says,
"Pray with faith"

Jesus said, "Have faith in God . . .
and you will be given
whatever you ask for."   Mark 11:22, 24

James Murdoch spent three weeks
in the White House as the guest
of President Abraham Lincoln.
One night, before the Battle of Bull Run,
Murdoch couldn't sleep.
Suddenly he heard moaning.
He went to see what it was. He writes:
"I saw the President
kneeling beside an open window.
His back was toward me. . . .
Then he cried out
in tones so pleading and sorrowful:
'O thou God that heard Solomon
on the night when he prayed for wisdom,
hear me; I cannot lead this people,
I cannot guide the affairs of this nation
without thy help.
I am poor, and weak, and sinful.
O God! . . . hear me and save this nation.'"
Emanuel Hertz, ed., *Lincoln Talks: A Biography in Anecdote*

Can I recall a time when I prayed from
the depths of my being, as Lincoln did here?

Prayer is an expression of who we are. . . .
We are a living incompleteness . . .
that calls for fulfillment.   Thomas Merton

Jesus says,
"Pray with confidence"

Jesus said, "You know how to give. . . .
How much more . . .
will the Father . . . give the Holy Spirit
to those who ask!"   Luke 11:13

Long ago, no rain fell and all life was dying.
One day a girl went up a mountain with a tin
dipper to seek water for her dying mother.
Returning, she gave a drink to a dying dog.
As she did, the dipper changed to silver
and refilled. Then she gave a drink to a man
who was so thirsty he could no longer speak.
The dipper turned to gold and refilled.
Arriving home, the girl gave the dipper
to her mother, who drank all she wanted.
Water still remained. The girl then gave a drink
to a stranger who came to the door.
One drop clung to the dipper.
As the girl took the dipper, the drop fell.
Where it hit the ground, a spring gushed up,
watering the whole land. In the excitement,
no one saw the stranger disappear.
But that night everyone saw
a "dipper of stars" sparkling in the sky.
It remains there to this very day.

In light of Jesus' words,
how might I interpret the "dipper" story?

God's gifts
put man's best dreams to shame.   E. B. Browning

Witness as Jesus did

An old story concerns
an elderly woman living with her son,
his wife, and their small daughter.
One day she began having accidents
at table, like spilling her coffee.

When the accidents became more frequent,
the son and his wife set up a little table
across the room in a corner.
There the woman ate alone off a bare table
that could be wiped easily after spills.

One day the couple
saw their daughter building something.
When they asked her what it was, she said,
"I'm building a little table for you to eat at
when I am grown up and married."

That night the couple let the elderly mother
return to the table.
And they were very kind to her,
even when she spilled her coffee.

[Jesus said to the people of his generation,
"How terrible for you if you] cause
one of these little ones to sin.
So watch what you do!"   Luke 17:1–3

Someone said of our modern generation,
"The worst danger that confronts
the younger generation is the example
set by the older generation."   E. C. McKenzie

This week's meditations
focus on the importance of witness.

Prayer procedure

You may wish to consider
ending each meditation this week
with this prayer to Jesus:

Shine through me and be so in me
that every soul I come in contact with
may feel your presence in my spirit.
                              John Henry Newman

Suggested daily readings

1 Jesus shines like the sun   Mt 17:1–8
2 Jesus is our light   Jn 12:20–36
3 Jesus is the real light   Jn 1:1–9
4 Jesus says, "Be a light, also"   Mt 5:13–16
5 Jesus says, "Fear not"   Mt 10:26–31
6 Jesus makes a promise   Mt 10:40–42
7 Jesus says, "Recast your nets"   Jn 21:1–13

Jesus' face
shines like the sun

*[Peter, James, and John
were on a mountain with Jesus.
Suddenly his face glowed like the sun.]
A shining cloud came over them,
and a voice from the cloud said,
"This is my own dear Son,
with whom I am pleased—listen to him!"*
                                    Matthew 17:5

The Book of Exodus says that when Moses
came down from Mount Sinai after talking
with God, "his face was shining."   Exodus 34:30
Somewhat similarly, an ancient letter says that
when Saint Elizabeth of Hungary came from prayer,
people often saw "her face shining marvelously
and light coming from her eyes
like rays from the sun."
It was this kind of "halo" phenomenon
that the disciples beheld in Jesus
on the mountain.

How well do I radiate the light of my faith
to those with whom I live and work?

*With our own eyes we saw his greatness.
We were there when . . . the voice
came to him from the Supreme Glory,
saying, "This is my own dear Son,
with whom I am pleased!"
We ourselves heard this voice . . .
on the holy mountain.*   2 Peter 1:16–18

Journal

Jesus says,
"Be people of the light"

Jesus said, "Believe in the light . . .
while you have it, so that you will be
the people of the light."   John 12:36

Anne Herbert was sitting in a restaurant
in Sausalito, California. Suddenly she took
a pencil from her purse and wrote down
a phrase she'd been mulling over for days.
Now you see the phrase on bumper stickers,
business cards, and at the bottom of letters.
One woman saw it spray-painted
on a warehouse 100 miles from her home.
When she got home, she tried to recall it
to write it down, but it wasn't quite right.
So she drove all the way back to copy it.
The phrase that appeals to so many reads:
"Practice random kindness
and senseless acts of beauty."
Anne believes that "random kindness"
can trigger a tidal wave of good in the world,
just as "random violence" triggers evil.
Maybe that's why you see the phrase everywhere.
It touches something deep in the heart;
it appeals to the very best in us.

What "random kindness" or "senseless act
of beauty" might I recklessly commit today?

Like all revolutions, guerrilla goodness
begins slowly, with a single act.
Let it be yours.   Glamour magazine

Jesus says,
"Let your light shine"

Journal

Jesus said,
"You are like light for the whole world."
Matthew 5:14

Dr. Robert Healy wrote a letter
to *Psychology Today* about a young man
who had entered therapy after near-suicide.
The man was driving to a bridge,
intending to leap off it.
Routinely, he stopped at a traffic light
and looked toward the sidewalk.
There on the curb stood an elderly lady,
who gave him the warmest,
most beautiful smile
he could ever remember receiving.
It was as if she knew that he needed it.
The light changed and he drove on.
But her smile drove away with him.
He said later that he had no idea
who she was; nor did he see her again.
He only knows he owes his life to her—
and to what her smile said to him
at the most critical moment of his life.

What keeps me from affirming others
more than I am currently doing?

I don't know
what the big deal is about age.
People who shine from the inside
look twenty years younger.   Singer Dolly Parton

Journal

Jesus says, "You are like light for the world"

Jesus said,
"Your light must shine before people,
so that they will . . . praise your Father."
Matthew 5:16

Many rural villages in India
are totally without electricity.
People use tiny oil lamps,
much like those used in Jesus' time,
to light their homes.
The temple in one of these rural villages
has a large frame hanging from its ceiling.
Cut into the frame are a hundred slots
into which tiny oil lamps can be placed.
When the people go to the temple after dark,
they carry their oil lamps from their homes
to guide them through the darkness.
Upon arriving in the temple,
they place the lamp in one of the slots
in the frame.
By the time the last villager arrives,
the darkness of the temple has been transformed
into a glorious sea of light.

What keeps me from being an even greater
contributor to the "glorious sea of light"
that Jesus asks his followers to be?

Every believer in this world
must become a spark of light.
Pope John XXIII

Jesus says, "Let people know you belong to me"

Jesus said,
"Those who declare publicly
that they belong to me,
I will do the same for them
before my Father in heaven."
Matthew 10:32

Tip O'Neill was a member of
the House of Representatives for 34 years.
In the memoirs of his political life,
Tip says that he'll never forget
a day in Missouri in 1960.
He was riding in an open car
in a campaign parade with Jack Kennedy.
He writes:
"Somebody mentioned that
in the neighborhood we were driving through
there was a good deal of concern
over the Catholic issue.
Then we passed a Catholic school,
with all the nuns standing outside,
holding their Kennedy signs.
'Stop the car,' said Jack. He got out
and shook hands with all the sisters,
and I loved him for it."

How ready am I to do what I think is right,
even if it means risking my popularity?

Who sells principles for popularity
is soon bankrupt. E. C. McKenzie (slightly adapted)

Journal

Jesus says, "I will bless those who help others"

Jesus said, "You can be sure that
whoever gives even a drink of cold water
to one of the least of these my followers
because he is my follower,
will certainly receive a reward."
                                    Matthew 10:42

A brutal scene in Victor Hugo's novel
Notre Dame of Paris shows Quasi Modo,
the hunchback, chained to a wheel
and being scourged before a huge mob.
As blood flows from his wounds,
he calls out pathetically for water.
The mob responds by jeering him and pelting
him with stones. Suddenly, a little girl
with a gourd of water in her hand
pushes through the crowd and gives him a drink.
The girl's loving action makes him do
what his torturers could not do.
A tear rolls down his cheek.

What do I imagine went on in the minds
of Quasi Modo and the mob as they watched
the little girl's compassionate act?

Yours are the only hands
with which God can do his work. . . .
Yours are the only eyes
through which God's compassion
can shine upon a troubled world.
                                    Saint Teresa of Avila

Jesus says, "Recast your net for a catch"

*[The disciples fished all night
and caught nothing. As they neared shore,
Jesus saw them and said,
"Recast your net." They did] and
could not pull it back in, because
they had caught so many fish.*   John 21:6

The career of novelist A. J. Cronin
almost ended before it began.
Halfway into his first book, *Hatter's Castle*
(now translated into 19 languages),
he became discouraged and tossed it
into the wastebasket.
Then he went outside into the rain
and walked down a lonely rural road.
He came upon an old farmer working alone
in the rain, ditching a huge field.
The sight of the farmer—not discouraged
by the size of the field or the rain—
inspired him to go back and try again.
Years later, he credited his brilliant career
to the farmer's silent inspiration.

Someone said, "Jesus spoke to Cronin
through that farmer, saying, "Recast your net
and try again." Can I recall Jesus ever speaking
to me through the silent witness of a friend
or a family member? Who? When?

Lighthouses blow no horns; they only shine.
Dwight L. Moody

Love as Jesus did

No bands played; no flags waved.
A car honked, and my son said,
"I guess that's for me."

He picked up his bag and kissed his mother.
Then he held out his hand and said, "So long."
I shook it and said, "Good luck, son!"
We walked him to the door.
We waved, and the car drove away.
Our son was off to war.

I said something to my wife to give me
an excuse to go upstairs to his room.
I sat down and thought,
"How quickly time has passed.
Only yesterday he was a just a little boy."
I also thought about how I saw him off.
I shook his hand and said, "Good luck."
Later, I would write these words:

"I wished that I had somehow been able
to tell him how much I really loved him. . . .
And I thought:
what fools we are with our children,
always plotting what we shall make of them,
never accepting what they are."
Retold in the first person

That was the last time
that Howard O'Brien ever saw his son.
He was killed shortly afterward in combat.

Why are so many of us like Howard O'Brien?
Perhaps Dale Carnegie put it best:

We are all dreaming of some magical
rose garden over the horizon—
instead of enjoying the roses
that are blooming
outside our windows today.

This week's meditations focus on
Jesus' teaching about love.
They invite us to imitate Jesus' love for us.

Suggested daily readings

1 Jesus talks about love		Mk 12:28–34
2 Jesus shows his love		Lk 7:11–17
3 Jesus talks of love signs		Lk 7:36–47
4 Jesus says, "Love children"		Mk 10:13–16
5 Jesus says, "Love everyone"		Lk 6:32–36
6 Jesus says, "Love as I love"		Jn 15:9–17
7 Jesus says, "Love your enemies"		Lk 6:27–31

Jesus says, "Love God with all your heart"

Jesus said,
" 'Love the Lord your God
with all your heart,
with all your soul, [and]
with all your mind.' "   Mark 12:30–31

Fifteen-year-old Therese Martin
entered the Carmelite convent in France.
From the day she entered,
she dreamed of doing "great" things for God.
The years passed without her dream
being even remotely realized.
Naturally, she was disappointed.
Then one day she was reading Saint Paul,
where he says the "best" way to holiness
is not doing "great" things for God,
but doing loving things.   1 Corinthians 12:31–13:13
After reading this, she wrote in her journal:
"O Jesus . . . at last I have found my calling:
my calling is to love."

This episode in the life
of Saint Therese of Lisieux
invites me to ask:
What are some of the loving things
that I have done for God in the past week?
The past 24 hours?

We cannot do great things,
only small things with great love.
                              Mother Teresa

Journal

_____
_____
_____
_____
_____
_____
_____
_____
_____
_____
_____
_____

Jesus says, "Love your neighbor as yourself"

Jesus said,
" 'Love the Lord your God. . . .'
This is the greatest
and the most important commandment.
The second most important commandment
is like it: 'Love your neighbor
as you love yourself.' "   Matthew 22:37–39

An old poem by an unknown poet
asks this question: What is love?
The poet responds by listing six answers.
They go something like this. "Love is:
silence—when words would hurt,
patience—when another's curt,
deafness—when another's mad,
gentleness—when another's sad,
promptness—when a need is seen,
courage—when life is mean."

Of the poet's examples of love,
which do I score highest on?
Lowest? Why?
What is one concrete thing I might do
to make my love more like Jesus' love?

What does love look like?
It has feet
to go to the poor and needy.
It has eyes to see misery and want.
It has ears to hear sighs and sorrows.
Saint Augustine

Jesus shows his love
for little children

Journal

Jesus took the children in his arms,
placed his hands on each of them,
and blessed them.   Mark 10:16

A skinny boy with a shoeshine kit
stood at the edge of a sidewalk cafe.
A woman felt a surge of admiration for him
for trying to be a man and earn a living.
Just then a man charged out of the cafe,
grabbed the boy, and threw him
like a bag of garbage into the street.
The boy held tightly to his kit
to keep its contents from flying all over.
The woman's heart went out to the boy.
Why did the man treat the boy so brutally?
The boy hadn't picked anybody's pocket.
He hadn't stolen anyone's purse.
He hadn't tried to sell drugs.
As he limped off, ashamed and humiliated,
the woman wondered:
How will this cruel experience affect
the boy's attitude toward work and people?
Will it snuff out
the tiny spark of initiative and hope
that once flickered in his hurt heart?

What might Jesus say to the boy? The man?

Jesus said, "If anyone should cause
one of these little ones to lose faith in me,
[woe to that person]."   Mark 9:42

Journal

Jesus says,
"Love everyone"

Jesus said,
"Why should God reward you
if you love only the people who love you?
Even the tax collectors do that!"

Matthew 5:46

Howard Whitman knew a doctor
who had been practicing medicine
with remarkable success for over 30 years.
One day the doctor told Howard:
"I've prescribed many different remedies
for many different kinds of ailments.
And after all these years and
after all those prescriptions,
I'm convinced that the best remedy
for what ails many people
is simply a generous dose of love."
Howard thought a minute and said,
"And what if that dose doesn't work?"
"Then, I'd double it," said the doctor.

What family member or friend needs
a double dose of love every day
for the next two weeks, at least?
How might I help to provide it?

The worst sin towards
our fellow creatures is not to hate them,
but to be indifferent to them;
that is the essence of inhumanity.

George Bernard Shaw

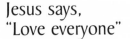

Jesus says, "The greatest love is to give your life"

Jesus said, "The greatest love you can have for your friends is to give your life for them." John 15:13

Each year Frank Gajounicezek
visits Auschwitz to lay a wreath on the bunker
where a priest named Maximillian Kolbe
died in his stead. It happened like this.
A prisoner escaped from the Nazi camp.
The next morning the camp commander
forced all the other prisoners to stand
all day in the blazing hot sun.
At 6 P.M.,
after many had fainted and were beaten,
he picked ten men at random
to die because of the escapee.
One was Gajounicezek. An eyewitness says:
"He screamed that he wanted to live to see
his wife and children. . . .
Then suddenly Father Kolbe . . .
stepped forward . . . to take the man's place.
In camps like Auschwitz it was unheard of
that somebody would die for another.
It restored our faith in the human race."

What was one of the most generous acts
that I freely chose to do in my life?

*The best use of life
is to spend it for something
that outlasts life.* William James

Journal

Journal

Jesus says, "Love even your enemies"

Jesus said, "You have heard that it was said,
'Love your friends, hate your enemies.'
But now I tell you: love your enemies."
Matthew 5:43–44

Abraham Lincoln succeeded Buchanan
as president in 1861.
Ed Stanton, a member of Buchanan's cabinet,
had nothing but disdain for Lincoln.
He ridiculed Lincoln publicly,
referring to him as the "original gorilla."
A year into the presidency,
Lincoln had to replace his Secretary of War.
He chose Stanton, explaining,
"I know the terrible things he said about me.
But he's the best man for the job."
Shortly after Lee surrendered to Grant,
Lincoln was assassinated.
One of the first public officials to reach
Lincoln's side was Stanton.
When Lincoln breathed his last,
Stanton said with heartfelt sincerity,
"There lies the world's greatest ruler.
Now he belongs to the ages."

How do I respond to ridicule? What keeps me
from responding as Lincoln did?

Without love and compassion for others,
our own apparent love for Christ
is fiction.   Thomas Merton

Jesus says, "Who receives the one I send welcomes me"

Jesus said,
"Whoever receives anyone I send
receives me also;
and whoever receives me
receives him who sent me." John 13:20

Ensworth Reisner remembers a minister
who had very little money.
He was just scraping by.
One day a destitute family came to him.
The minister was moved to pity
and gave them
all the money he had on hand.
Then, as they left, he said,
"Thank you for the privilege
of letting me help you."
Reisner says, "Those remarkable words
taught me an important lesson.
When people give you the opportunity
to help them, they give you the opportunity
to be like God.
And for that we should give them thanks."

What keeps me from having the same attitude
that Ensworth Reisner has?

God has given us two hands—
one to receive with
and the other to give with.
We are not made cisterns for hoarding;
we are channels made for sharing. Billy Graham

Journal

_____

_____

_____

_____

_____

_____

_____

_____

_____

_____

_____

_____

_____

Serve as Jesus did

Abraham Lincoln
began his historic career as a lawyer
in Springfield, Illinois.

One morning
he walked into the bank looking a mess.
His shoes, socks, and pants legs
were all dripping wet.
The banker, who knew him well,
laughed and said,
"What happened to you?"

"Well," said Lincoln, "there was
this little girl on her way to school.
She was pretty wet from the storm
and was trying to figure out
how to get across the flooded street.
Obviously, she needed help.
So I put my hands under her arms,
waded through the flood water,
and set her down on the other side."

This week's meditations
focus on the importance of service.
They invite us to imitate Jesus,
who said:

*"The Son of Man . . .
did not come to be served,
but to serve and to give his life
to redeem many people."*   Matthew 20:28

Suggested prayer procedure

You might consider
concluding each meditation this week
with this prayer to Jesus:

*Lord, teach me to be generous.
Teach me to serve you as your deserve;
to give and not to count the cost;
to fight and not to heed the wounds;
to toil and not to seek for rest;
to labor and not to ask for reward,
except to know
that I am doing your will.*
Prayer of Saint Ignatius of Loyola

Suggested daily readings

1	Jesus talks of serving others	Mk 9:33–37
2	Jesus feeds the hungry	Jn 6:1–13
3	Jesus says, "Help the needy"	Mt 25:31–46
4	Jesus talks about duty	Lk 17:7–10
5	Jesus tells a service parable	Lk 10:32–35
6	Jesus talks about giving	Mt 6:1–4
7	Jesus praises a widow's gift	Mk 12:41–44

Jesus says, "The first should serve the rest"

Jesus sat down, called the twelve disciples,
and said to them,
"Whoever wants to be first
must place himself last of all
and be the servant of all."   Mark 9:35

Twice a year geese migrate
in a beautiful V formation, as a flock.
Philip Yancey explains: "That's the secret
of their strength. . . . Cooperating as a flock,
geese can fly at 71 percent longer range. . . .
The lead goose cuts a swath through the
air resistance, which creates a helping uplift
for the two birds behind him.
In turn, their beating makes it easier
on the birds behind them. . . .
Each bird takes his turn as the leader.
The tired ones fan out to the edges of the V
for a breather, and the rested ones
surge forward to the point of the V
to drive the flock onward."   *Campus Life* magazine
Yancey says that if a goose becomes sick
and needs to rest, another goose will
stay with it until it can continue again.

How ready am I to place myself
at the service of all, especially the needy?

O God, help us to be masters of ourselves
that we may be servants of others.
Sir Alec Paterson

Journal

_____

_____

_____

_____

_____

_____

_____

_____

_____

_____

Jesus says, "Try to do God's will, as I try to do it"

Jesus said,
"I am not trying to do what I want,
but only what he who sent me wants."
John 5:30

A plaque in London contains these words:
"To the memory
of Charles Gordon
Who at all times and everywhere
gave
His Strength to the Weak
His Substance to the Poor
His Sympathy to the Suffering
His Heart to God."
Whether the plaque's author knew it or not,
he was describing the heart of Jesus.
No finer tribute could be paid to a person.

Can I recall some recent occasion
when I went out of my way to help—
someone weaker than myself,
someone poorer than myself,
someone suffering more than myself?

I am only one, but still I am one.
I cannot do everything,
but still I can do something;
and because I cannot do everything,
let me not refuse
to do the something that I can do.
Edward Everett Hale

Jesus says, "What you do to the least, you do to me"

Journal

*[Jesus said, "At the last judgment,
people will say to the King,]
'When, Lord, did we ever see you . . .
a stranger and welcome you in our homes,
or naked and clothe you? . . .'
The King will reply,
'I tell you, whenever you did this
for one of the least important of these . . .
you did it for me!' "* Matthew 25:37–38, 40

In 1952 Mother Teresa
saw an abandoned woman in the street,
literally being eaten by bugs.
She carried the unfortunate victim
to a hospital, but it wouldn't accept her.
Next, Mother Teresa carried the woman
to city officials, demanding she be helped.
When this didn't work, she demanded
a shelter where she could care for
the woman and other victims like her.
Glad to be rid of the problem,
they led her to an abandoned shelter,
once used by Hindu pilgrims.
Thus began Mother Teresa's first home
for the destitute and the dying.

How can I become more involved in helping
people who cannot help themselves?

*Service is nothing but love
in work clothes.* E. C. McKenzie

Journal

Jesus says, "When we serve, we are only doing our duty"

[Jesus said to his disciples,]
"When you have done
all you have been told to do, say,
'We are ordinary servants;
we have only done our duty.' "   Luke 17:10

The great physicist Albert Einstein
notes that our situation on earth is strange.
We come for a short span of time,
not knowing for certain why we are here,
but seemingly with a divine purpose.
Then he makes this surprising statement:
"From the standpoint of daily life . . .
there is one thing we know.
That we are here for the sake of others . . .
for the countless unknown souls
with whose fate we are connected. . . .
Many times a day, I realize how much
my own outer and inner life is built upon
the labors of people, both living and dead,
and how earnestly I must exert myself
in order to give in return
as much as I have received."

From what three people have I received much?
What was it? How can I return it?

Happiness will never be ours
if we do not recognize to some degree
that God's blessings were given us
for the well-being of all.   Anonymous

Jesus says, "Give to the needy without any fanfare"

Jesus said,
"When you help a needy person,
do it in such a way
that even your closest friend
will not know about it."   Matthew 6:3

The *New York Times* ran this amazing story.
Tammie Murphy, donations clerk at St. Jude's
Children's Research Hospital in Memphis,
gets about 700 donation envelopes daily.
One day she opened a plain envelope with
no return address. Inside was a McDonald's
Monopoly Sweepstake's card.
It showed a $1 million "Instant Winner."
The hospital called McDonald's.
Officials came with a representative
of the Arthur Andersen accounting firm.
After checking the card with a jeweler's eyepiece,
he declared it a winner.
McDonald's and St. Jude officials agreed
to respect the donor's apparent desire
to remain anonymous.
They made no effort to find out who it was.
Later, the *Reader's Digest* ran the story
in the magazine's feature "Heroes for Today."

When was the last time I gave generously—
and anonymously—to a good cause?

Love inspires heroism;
heroism inspires imitation.   Anonymous

Journal

Jesus praises the gift of a poor widow

[Seeing a poor widow drop into the Temple treasury a few small coins, Jesus said, "She gave more] than all the others. . . . She gave all she had to live on." Mark 12:43–44

Eric Zorn, a *Chicago Tribune* columnist, couldn't believe what he saw. Dennis Dunn, dressed in a blue sport coat and holding a coffee can, was begging money from winos on Chicago's West Side. Dunn explained that he was working for Making Choices, a prison ministry. It provides guidance and social support for youth released from a detention center. To get to meetings, they have to cross gang boundaries. The ministry needed a van to pick them up. Most of the funds came from suburbanites, but Dunn thought people in the area wanted to feel a part of the ministry. "A waitress at Edna's Soul Food Restaurant . . . emptied her tip apron. . . . A guy with his bottle in a bag tossed in a pair of dimes." Dunn said, "No matter what you've heard . . . these neighborhoods are filled with people who care." Even the winos. Unbelievable.

What two things in this story spoke to me in a special way?

As the purse is emptied the heart is filled.
Victor Hugo

Jesus says, "Invite the needy; God will repay you"

Journal

Jesus said, "When you give a feast,
invite the poor, the crippled, the lame,
and the blind; and you will be blessed,
because they are not able to pay you back.
God will repay you."   Luke 14:13–14

There's a scene in Frank Capra's movie
Mr. Deeds Goes to Town in which Gary Cooper
explains his concern for the poor.
He says:
"There will always be leaders and followers.
It's like the road out in front of my house.
It's on a steep hill.
And every day I watch the cars climbing up.
Some go lickety-split up that hill in high—
some have to shift into second—
and some sputter and shake and
slip back to the bottom again. . . .
And I say that the fellas who can make
the hill in high should help those who can't.
That's all I'm trying to do with this money.
Help the fellas
who can't make the hill in high."

Concretely, how am I showing concern for
"the fellas who can't make the hill in high"?

Happy are those
who are concerned for the poor;
the Lord will help them
when they are in trouble.   Psalms 41:1

Forgive as Jesus did

Dag Hammarskjöld, UN secretary-general,
was killed in a plane crash
while en route to Africa
to try to negotiate a cease-fire.

Later, his personal journal, *Markings,*
was found in his New York apartment.
Hammarskjöld identified it as a
"sort of *white book* concerning
my negotiations with myself
and with God." One entry reads:

Who "forgives" you—out of love—
takes upon himself the consequences
of what you have done. . . . The price
you must pay for your own liberation . . .
is that you in turn must be willing
to liberate in the same way irrespective
of the consequences to yourself.

Hammarskjöld was simply underscoring
Jesus' teaching:
to forgive others as Jesus forgives us.
An example of the "price" this can entail
is illustrated in the case of a father
whose son was brutally murdered.
The father's grief and the family's grief
weighed on their hearts like a rock.
After deep meditation and prayer,
the father picked up a pencil
and wrote:

O God,
we remember not only our son
but also his murderers . . .
because through their crime
we now follow thy footsteps more closely
in the way of sacrifice. . . .
So when his murderers stand before thee on
the day of judgment, remember and forgive.

This week's meditations
deal with that part of the Lord's Prayer
that we pray daily
but usually fail to reflect on sufficiently:
asking God to forgive us
as we forgive others.

Suggested daily readings

1 Jesus forgives a man's sins　　　Mk 2:1–12

2 Jesus forgives a woman's sins　　Jn 8:1–11

3 Jesus' unforgiving servant story　Mt 18:21–35

4 Jesus stresses forgiveness　　　Mt 6:9–15

5 Jesus' prodigal son parable　　　Lk 15:11–32

6 Jesus lost coin parable　　　　Lk 15:8–10

7 Jesus' lost sheep parable　　　Lk 15:1–7

Jesus forgives
the sins of a man

*[Some people brought a paralytic to Jesus
to be healed.] Seeing how much faith
they had, Jesus said to the paralyzed man,
"My son, your sins are forgiven."
[At once the man was healed.]*   Mark 2:5

Harold Hughes described himself as
"a drunk, a liar, and a cheat."
He was so convinced he'd never change
that he decided to end it all.
At the last moment, however,
he remembered enough from the Bible
to realize that to take one's life was wrong.
So he knelt down sobbing and explained
to God why he was going to end it all.
Suddenly, something happened
that he never experienced before in his life.
He wrote later:
"God was reaching down and touching me.
Like a stricken child lost in a storm,
I suddenly stumbled into the warm hands
of my Father. Joy filled me, so intense
it seemed to burst my breast."
Ten years later, Harold Hughes
was elected governor of Iowa.

When did I, perhaps, feel God "touching me"?

*Jesus said,
"Happy are those who mourn;
God will comfort them!"*   Matthew 5:4

Journal

_____

_____

_____

_____

_____

_____

_____

_____

_____

_____

_____

_____

Jesus says, "I have come to call sinners and outcasts"

*[Some Pharisees criticized Jesus
for eating with sinners.
Jesus replied,]
"People who are well do not need a doctor,
but only those who are sick. . . .
I have not come to call respectable people,
but outcasts."*   Matthew 9:12–13

Presidential aide Charles Colson
was sent to prison for his role
in the Watergate scandal. Speaking to 900
prisoners in Atlanta, Colson said bluntly,
"Jesus Christ came into this world
for the poor, the sick, the hungry,
the homeless, the imprisoned.
He is the Prophet of the loser.
And all of us assembled here are losers.
I am a loser just like every one of you.
The miracle is that God's message is
specifically for those of us
who have failed."   Charles Colson, *Life Sentence*
Once out of prison, Colson set up the Prison
Fellowship Program, which involves 1,200
volunteers and reaches into 500 prisons.

Which of the following groups do I help
most and least and why: the poor, the sick,
the hungry, the homeless, the imprisoned?

*I am truly poor, not when I have nothing,
but when I do nothing.*   Anonymous

Jesus says, "Forgive others as God forgives you"

[Jesus told a parable about an official who owed a huge debt to a king. When the official begged for mercy, the king forgave his entire debt. Incredibly, the official left and refused to show similar mercy to a fellow servant. The king heard about this and punished the official severely, saying,] "You should have had mercy on your fellow servant, just as I had mercy on you."   Matthew 18:33

A mother pleaded with Napoleon to pardon her son for an offense. Napoleon said, "This is his second offense; justice demands he be severely punished." The mother said, "I'm not asking for justice; I'm asking for mercy." Napoleon said, "Your son does not deserve mercy." "Sir," the mother said, "if he deserved it, it wouldn't be mercy. I'm asking for mercy." At this, the French general said, "I will show him mercy."

How merciful am I toward people in my thoughts, words, and actions? What might help me be more merciful?

Teach me to feel another's woe, To hide the fault I see; That mercy I to others show, That mercy show to me.   Alexander Pope

Journal

_____

_____

_____

_____

_____

_____

_____

_____

_____

_____

_____

_____

Journal

Jesus says, "Forgive seventy times seven times"

*[Peter asked Jesus,] "How many times
do I have to forgive . . . ? Seven times?" . . .
Jesus said, "Seventy times seven."*
Matthew 18:21–22

William Barclay, the Scottish theologian,
tells the story of Tokichi Ishii,
whose cruelty and brutality were legendary.
When Ishii was awaiting execution,
two religious people tried to talk to him.
He "glowered back at them," like an animal.
They managed to leave a Bible, however.
Later, Ishii began to read it. When he came
to the crucifixion, he was stunned
by the words, "Father, forgive them,
for they know not what they do." He says,
"I was stabbed to the heart, as if pierced
by a five-inch nail. Shall I call it the love
of Christ? Shall I call it compassion?
I do not know. . . . I only know that I believed
and the hardness of my heart was changed."
Daily Celebration

How ready am I to forgive
"seventy times seven" times?
What do I do if I find it hard?

*We are like beasts when we kill.
We are like human beings when we judge.
We are like God when we forgive.*
Anonymous

Jesus says,
"Forgive from your heart"

Jesus said,
"Forgive . . . from your heart."   Matthew 18:35

A moving scene from
All Quiet on the Western Front portrays
a German soldier in a shell hole,
taking cover from artillery fire.
Suddenly, an enemy French soldier leaps
into the same hole to take cover.
The German pounces on him and stabs him.
But the Frenchman doesn't die immediately.
The German—hardly more than a boy—
studies the French soldier's dying eyes.
Moved to pity, he makes him comfortable
and gives him a drink from his own canteen.
When the Frenchman dies minutes later,
the young German feels great remorse.
He speaks to the dead Frenchman, saying:
"When you jumped in here,
you were my enemy—and I was afraid. . . .
But you're just a man like me,
and I killed you. . . . O God! Why did they . . .
send us out to fight each other?
If we threw away these rifles and
these uniforms, you could be my brother. . . .
You have to forgive me."

What are my thoughts on the above scene?

Forgiveness is the fragrance a violet sheds
on the heel that has crushed it.   Mark Twain

117

Journal

Jesus says, "One sin alone cannot be forgiven"

Jesus said, "Whoever says a word against the Son of Man can be forgiven; but whoever says evil things against the Holy Spirit will not be forgiven." Luke 12:10

A speaker kept insisting on the need to continue to reach out to teenagers. During the question-and-answer period, a mother asked, "But what do you do if you keep reaching out to teenagers and they keep pushing you away and even speak against you to their friends?" This seems to be what Jesus is referring to in this passage. When people reject him and speak against him, all Jesus can do is to continue to reach out to them. Hopefully, after he returns to the Father, and the Holy Spirit comes, they will see the light and accept salvation. But if they also reject the Holy Spirit, then even God's hands are tied. Salvation—like love—is a gift. No one— not even God—can force it on a person.

In what way might I be tying God's hands when it comes to receiving salvation

If God is kept outside, something must be wrong inside. E. C. McKenzie

Jesus carries home the lost sheep

[Jesus said, "When you find a lost sheep,]
you are so happy
that you put it on your shoulders
and carry it back home." Luke 15:5–6

George Vest's "Eulogy of a Dog" reads in part:
"He guards the sleep of his pauper master
as if he were a prince.
When all other friends desert, he remains.
When riches take wings . . .
he is as constant in his love as the sun
in its journey though the heavens.
If fortune drives the master forth an outcast
in the world, friendless and homeless . . .
the faithful dog asks no higher privilege
than that of accompanying him. . . .
And when . . . death takes the master . . .
there by his graveside will the noble dog
be found, his head between his paws . . .
faithful and true even to death."
Congressional Record (October 16, 1914)

The loyalty of a dog and that of a shepherd
are faint images of Jesus' loyalty to me.
How well do these images reflect
my own loyalty and faithfulness to Jesus—
and to those to whom I owe much?

Never let go of loyalty and faithfulness.
Tie them around your neck;
write them on your heart. Proverbs 3:3

Journal

Watch and pray

Ancient weddings lasted for days.
A high point was the arrival
of the groom at the bride's home.
There, young women with lighted oil lamps
waited to escort him inside.

It is against this background that
Jesus told the parable of ten young women.
Five are wise and have a full supply of oil.
Five are foolish and have a small supply.
When the bridegroom delays in coming,
they all fall asleep.
At midnight, they awake to the shout,
"The bridegroom is on his way!"

The five foolish young women discover,
to their dismay, that they have no oil left.
So they rush off to get some.
While they are gone, the groom arrives.
The five who were ready
escort him into the wedding feast,
and the door is closed.
The five foolish women are locked out.

Jesus used this parable to teach
that after he returns to heaven,
he will come back again in glory
at an hour when we will least expect him.
Therefore, we must be ready always!
Only those who are ready
will enter the wedding feast with him.

Only those who are ready
will hear him say the joyful words:

*"Come and possess the kingdom
which has been prepared for you
ever since the creation of the world."*
Matthew 25:34

This week's meditations focus on
the return of Jesus and
the need to be prepared for it.
For some Jesus will come
at the end of their personal life.
For others he will come at the end of time.

Suggested daily readings

1 Jesus speaks of his return   Lk 21:25–28
2 Jesus speaks of end-time signs   Lk 21:7–19
3 Jesus speaks of the end time   Mt 24:29–31
4 Jesus says, "Be ready"   Mt 24:36–44
5 Jesus' parable of ten women   Mt 25:1–13
6 Jesus speaks about vigilance   Lk 12:35–40
7 Jesus says, "Pray for strength"   Lk 21:34–36

Jesus says of the last days,
"Strange things will happen"

Jesus said,
"There will be strange things happening
to the sun, the moon, and the stars. . . .
Then the Son of Man will appear, coming
in a cloud with great power and glory.
When these things begin to happen,
stand up and raise your heads,
because your salvation is near."   Luke 21:25, 27–28

Near the end of *The Great Dictator,*
Charlie Chaplin cries out:
"Hannah, can you hear me?
Wherever you are, look up, Hannah!
The clouds are lifting!
We are coming out of the darkness
into the light. We are coming
into a new world—a kindlier world,
where men will rise above their hate
and their greed and brutality.
Look up! Hannah!
The soul of man has been given wings,
and at last he is beginning to fly.
He is flying to the rainbow—
into the light of hope—
into the future—the glorious future
that belongs to you—to me—
and to all of us! Look up! Hannah! Look up!"

How eagerly do I await Jesus' return?

Come, Lord Jesus!   Revelation 22:20

Journal

Jesus says, "Kingdoms will attack one another"

Jesus said,
"Kingdoms will attack one another.
There will be . . . terrifying things
coming from the sky.
[But the end is not yet.]" Luke 21:10–11

Writing on scraps of scorched paper,
Dr. Michihibo Hachiya described Hiroshima
after the atomic bomb
killed a hundred thousand people
and left an equal number to die slowly.
Dazed people moved about
like scarecrows—their burnt arms
held away from their burnt body
to keep the two raw surfaces
from rubbing together painfully.
Blistering hot winds whipped
"dust and ashes into our eyes and noses.
Our mouths became dry, our throats raw. . . .
Coughing was uncontrollable."
Dead bodies were everywhere,
like "some giant had flung them
to their death from a great height. . . .
Hiroshima was no longer a city."
It had become a hell on earth.

What are my thoughts as I imagine myself
to be Dr. Hachiya?

Wrong rules the land,
and waiting justice sleeps. Josiah G. Holland

Jesus says, "The Son of Man will return suddenly"

Jesus said,
"Soon after the trouble of those days . . .
the sign of the Son of Man will appear . . .
on the clouds of heaven
with power and great glory.
The great trumpet will sound,
and he will send out his angels
to the four corners of the earth,
and they will gather his chosen people
from one end of the world to the other."

Matthew 24:29–31

Linda Taylor was shepherding
her three tiny tots upstairs to bed.
Peggy, who had just begun kindergarten,
stopped and said, "Mommy,
if the world ended right now . . ."
Linda gulped and said a quick prayer to God
for guidance. "Yes, Peggy," she said, "go on."
Peggy completed her question, asking,
"Would I have to take my library book back,
or would it be okay to leave it at home?"

How seriously do I take Jesus' teachings,
especially about the goal of this life?

What you possess in the world
will be found at the day of your death
to belong to another,
but what you are will be yours forever.

Henry Van Dyke

123

Journal

_____

_____

_____

_____

_____

_____

_____

_____

_____

_____

Jesus says, "I will return when you least expect"

Jesus said, "If the owner of a house knew the time when the thief would come, you can be sure that he would stay awake and not let the thief break into his house. So then, you also must always be ready, because the Son of Man will come at an hour when you are not expecting him."
Matthew 24:43–44

A retired woman invested her life's savings
in a business deal presented to her
by a clever young con artist.
When she discovered the awful truth,
she phoned the Better Business Bureau.
The spokesperson for the bureau asked,
"Why didn't you consult us before handing over
your money? Didn't you know that's why
we exist—to identify these thieves for you?"
"Yes, I knew," said the woman,
"but the young man looked so honest
that I didn't think it necessary in this case."

Jesus used the example of the "thief"
to dramatize the need for me to be ready
for the end of the world or
for the end of my own life in the world—
whichever comes first. How ready am I?

Get ready for eternity.
You are going to spend a lot of time there.
E. C. McKenzie

Jesus says, "No one knows the time of the return"

*Jesus said, "The Kingdom of heaven
will be like this. [Ten young women were
waiting at the bride's house for the groom.
He was tardy and night fell. Result?
They dozed and five missed his arrival.]"
Jesus concluded, "Watch out, then, because
you do not know the day or the hour
[of the Son of Man's return]."* Matthew 25:1, 13

The *Titanic* sank on April 14, 1912.
The *Washington Post* described this episode:
"In the wheelroom, a nattily uniformed officer
hummed at his task. . . .
The phone rang. A minute passed!
Another minute! The officer was busy!
The third precious minute passed.
The officer, his trivial task completed,
stepped to a phone. From the 'crow's nest'—
'Iceberg dead ahead! Reverse engines!'
But too late. As he rushed to the controls,
the 'pride of the seas' crashed
into the iceberg amid a deafening roar.
Three precious minutes!
Attention to trivial details and
six hundred people paid with their lives."

In what sense, perhaps, am I humming away
precious minutes on earth?

*All the treasures of earth cannot bring back
one lost moment.* French proverb

Journal

125

Journal

_____

_____

_____

_____

_____

_____

_____

_____

_____

_____

_____

Jesus says, "Happy are they who are ready on that day"

Jesus said,
"How happy are those servants
whose master finds them awake and ready
when he returns!" Luke 12:37

Sandra, on an early lunch break,
was phoning from a restaurant.
An older woman was sitting nearby.
Sandra said, "Mr. Bell, please."
When Mr. Bell answered, Sandra said,
"I hear that you're looking for an assistant."
There was a pause. Sandra replied,
"Oh! You say you hired one two weeks ago?
And you're very pleased with her?
Thank you." With that, Sandra hung up.
The woman said, "I couldn't help but hear.
Sorry you didn't get the job."
Sandra replied cheerfully,
"Thank you, but it's okay!
You see, Mr. Bell hired me two weeks ago
as his assistant, and I was wondering
what he thought of my work so far."

Jesus' words about his return and the story
of Sandra invite me to ask, If I could ask Jesus
right now what he thought of my work
on earth so far, what might he say?

It is not only what we do,
but also what we do not do,
for which we are held accountable. Molière

Jesus says, "Pray for strength to withstand that day"

Jesus said,
"Pray always that you will have
the strength to go safely
through all those things . . . and to stand
before the Son of Man." Luke 21:36

A very young man in a military hospital
had lost a leg and was sinking rapidly.
Lincoln happened by, saw him, and
offered to write a letter to his mother.
When the boy finished dictating it,
Lincoln added this postscript:
"This letter was written by A. Lincoln."
When the boy read the finished letter
and saw the postscript,
he gazed at Lincoln and asked,
"Are you our president?"
The president nodded. Then Lincoln added,
"Is there anything else I can do for you?"
The boy said feebly, "I guess you might
hold my hand and see me through."

What struck me most in this story?

I shall pass through this world but once.
Any good therefore that I can do,
or any kindness that I can show
to any human being, let me do it now.
Let me not defer it or neglect it,
for I shall not pass this way again.
Attributed to Stephen Grellet

Be prepared

An old poem
concerns the "last day of the world."
It describes a cross appearing in the sky.
From it shines a blood-red light.

The amazing thing about the light is
that it reveals people as they are.
It shines through the dungarees
of an oil-field worker
and reveals what is inside his heart.
It shines through the casual attire
of a college girl
and shows what is inside her soul.

The point of the poem
is that Jesus' return
will be followed by a judgment
that will reveal what we have become
in the course of our lives on earth.

It is against this backdrop
that Jesus told a parable about a merchant
who was departing on a long trip.
Before setting off,
he gave each of his three servants
sums of money to invest
and earn a profit during his absence.

Two servants turned an excellent profit
and were rewarded handsomely.
The third servant, however,

did nothing with his money and
was dismissed and punished.   Matthew 25:14–30

The point of the parable is clear.
Jesus instructs us that during
the time of his ascension to heaven
and his return,
we are to use our God-given talents
to advance the Kingdom of God on earth.
Following his return, Jesus will judge us
on how well we did this.

This week's meditations
focus on this judgment that will take place
upon Jesus' return.

Suggested daily readings

1 Jesus' wheat/weed parable   Mt 13:24–30
2 Jesus explains the parable   Mt 13:36–43
3 Jesus' three-servant parable   Mt 25:14–30
4 Jesus weeps over Jerusalem   Lk 19:41–44
5 Jesus' great-feast parable   Lk 14:15–24
6 Jesus says, "Be dressed"   Mt 22:1–14
7 Jesus' last-judgment parable   Mt 25:31–46

Jesus speaks about
the day of judgment

*[Jesus said, "God's Kingdom is like this.
One night an enemy sowed weeds
in a farmer's wheat field. When the farmer
learned of this, he said to his workers,]
"Let the wheat and the weeds both grow
together until harvest. Then I will tell the
harvest workers to pull up the weeds . . .
and burn them."*   Matthew 13:30

James Michener wrote an introduction
to A. Grove Day's book *Rascals in Paradise*.
In it he tells how a learned Australian saw
World War II coming. He checked a world atlas
for a safe haven to be when war came.
He chose an obscure island in the Pacific.
One week before Hitler invaded Poland,
he moved to his safe haven, Gaudalcanal.
As fate would have it,
it was destined to become the site
of one of the bloodiest battles of the war.
The point? In today's world there are no
more safe havens. The darkness of evil
will shadow us no matter where we go.

The pervasive presence of evil
leaves us with two options:
to curse the darkness or to light a candle.
What candle might I light?

Don't bunt. Aim out of the ballpark.
                        David Ogilvy

Journal

Jesus says, "Good and bad will be separated"

Jesus said,
"The Kingdom of heaven is like this.
Some fishermen throw their net out
in the lake and catch all kinds of fish.
When the net is full, they pull it to shore
and sit down to divide the fish:
the good ones go into the buckets,
the worthless ones are thrown away.
It will be like this
at the end of the age."   Matthew 13:47–49

Albert Schweitzer was a concert pianist
who gave up his career in music
to become a missionary doctor in Africa.
He once said, "It's not enough to say,
'I'm a good father. I'm a good husband.' . . .
You must do something . . .
for those who have need of help,
something for which you get no pay
but the privilege of doing it.
For remember, you don't live
in a world all your own.
Your brothers and sisters are here too."

What am I doing to help the needy outside
my circle of family and friends?

[On judgment day,]
God will not look you over
for medals, degrees or diplomas,
but for scars.   Elbert Hubbard

Jesus says, "All will be rewarded or punished"

Jesus said,
"The Kingdom of heaven will be like this. . . .
A man was about to leave home
on a trip; he called his servants
and put them in charge of his property.
He gave to each [a sum of money to invest.
At his return, he rewarded or punished
each according to how industriously
he had invested and used the money]."

Matthew 25:14–15

In his book *Souls on Fire,*
Elie Wiesel invites us to think about
using our talents a different way
than we ordinarily use them.
He says that when we meet our Creator,
we won't be asked,
"How well did you use the talents I gave you
to do great things for my people on earth?"
Rather, we'll be asked,
"How well did you use your talents
to become *you?*"

How would I respond to this question
if my Maker asked it of me this very night?

A rose only becomes beautiful
and blesses others when it opens and blooms.
Its greatest tragedy
is to stay in a tight-closed bud,
never fulfilling its potential.   Anonymous

Journal

Jesus says, "Stay committed; don't look back"

*[Jesus compared the Kingdom of God
to a great feast that a man prepared
for his son.] "When it was time . . .
he sent his servants to tell his guests,
'Come, everything is ready!'
But they all began, one after another,
to make excuses."* Luke 14:17–18

Greg was a promising young businessman.
He had one serious flaw, however.
He found it impossible to give a clear-cut
"yes" or "no" on certain critical issues.
Finally, the company arranged for him
to see a psychiatrist.
After greeting Greg, the psychiatrist said,
"I understand you
are having trouble making decisions."
Puzzled, Greg looked at the psychiatrist
and said, "Well, yes—and no!"

Jesus' parable highlights the need
for clear-cut commitment to God's Kingdom.
There is no room for procrastination.
What keeps me, perhaps,
from clear-cut, total commitment
to Jesus and to the work of bringing forth
the Kingdom of God on earth?

*Jesus said, "Anyone who starts to plow
and then keeps looking back
is of no use for the Kingdom of God."* Luke 9:62

Jesus says, "Those who are now last will be first"

*Jesus said, "People will come from
the east and the west, from the north
and the south, and sit down at the feast
in the Kingdom of God.
Then those who are now last will be first,
and those who are now first will be last."*
Luke 13:29–30

A death scene in *The Magnificent Ambersons*
touches on Jesus' warning. It reads:
"And now Major Amberson was engaged
in the profoundest thinking of his life,
and he realized that everything
that had worried or delighted him
during his lifetime—all his buying and
building and trading and banking—
that it was all a trifle and a waste
beside what concerned him now,
for the major knew now that he had to plan
to enter an unknown country
where he was not even sure
of being recognized as an Amberson."

What are my thoughts about my life
as I imagine myself to be Major Amberson?

*When his cold hand touches yours . . .
he will lead you away from
your investments . . . and real estate,
and with him you will pass into eternity. . . .
You will not be too busy to die.* A. E. Kittredge

Journal

Journal

Jesus says, "Repent and do good deeds"

Jesus said, "The Kingdom of heaven
is like this. Once there was a king
who prepared a wedding feast for his son. . . .
The king went in to look at the guests
and saw a man
who was not wearing wedding clothes.
[He expelled him.]" Matthew 22:2, 11

Ignace Lepp became a Communist, saying,
"I felt no need of God."
Then two things happened: Communism
turned sour and Lepp began to question
the meaning and purpose of life. He writes:
"It didn't seem logical that beings endowed
with a capacity for thinking and loving
could be thrown into an absurd universe,
where there was nothing to think,
nothing to love, and nothing to hope for."

The story of Ignace Lepp's conversion
helps us better understand Jesus' parable.
The wedding feast stands for God's *Kingdom;*
the wedding garment stands for *repentance*
(conversion accompanied by *good works*)—
the conditions for entry into the Kingdom.
What keeps me from complete conversion?

Mere sorrow, which weeps and sits still,
is not repentance. Repentance is sorrow
converted into action—into movement
toward a new and better life. Marvin Vincent

Jesus says, "What you do for the least you do for me"

[At the Last Judgment the King will say,]
"I was sick and you took care of me,
in prison and you visited me. . . .
I tell you, whenever you did this
for one of the least important . . .
you did it for me!" Matthew 25:36, 40

Tip O'Neill was a member of Congress
for thirty-four years.
He was speaker of the House for ten years,
the longest consecutive term
for any speaker in the history of Congress.
On the wall of his office
hung these words from the last speech
that Hubert Humphrey ever gave.
Tip said they summed up his own
"philosophy and values."
"The moral test of government
is how it treats those
who are in the dawn of life,
the children;
those who are in the twilight of life,
the aged; and
those who are in the shadows of life,
the sick, the needy, and the handicapped."

How do I treat these three groups?

By having reverence for life,
we enter into a spiritual relationship
with the world. Albert Schweitzer

Journal

135

Jesus is rejected

Toward the end of his life
Martin Luther King Jr. warned his followers:
"We've got some difficult days ahead.
But it doesn't matter with me now. . . .
I just want to do God's will."

Dr. King's words are similar to the warning
that Jesus gave his followers near the end
of his life:
"The Son of Man will be handed
over to those who will kill him."   Mark 9:31

The people to whom Jesus was referring
were the Jewish religious leaders.
Their hostility toward him
had been escalating steadily.

It began early in Jesus' ministry when
Jesus told a man,
"Your sins are forgiven."
When the leaders heard this, they grew
angry and shouted, "Blasphemy!
God is the only one who can forgive sins!"
       Mark 2:7

The hostility began to grow when Jesus
began working miracles on the Sabbath.
The leaders thought this violated God's law.

The hostility grew more and more serious
as more and more outcasts and sinners
began to follow Jesus.

Finally, the hostility reached the breaking
point when Jesus raised Lazarus to life.
At that point, the leaders met with the
Jewish High Council to decide what to do.

They said, "Look at all the miracles
this man is performing!
If we let him go on in this way,
everyone will believe in him." . . .
From that day on the Jewish authorities
made plans to kill Jesus.   John 11:47–48, 53

This week's meditations focus on
the escalating hostility between
Jesus and the Jewish religious leaders.

Suggested daily readings

1 Jesus meets opposition   Jn 8:31–47
2 Jesus' life is threatened   Jn 8:48–59
3 Jesus is rejected   Jn 10:22–39
4 Jesus' vineyard-tenant parable   Mk 12:1–12
5 Jesus talks about his death   Mk 8:31–38
6 Jesus makes a promise   Jn 8:12–20
7 Jesus is marked for death   Jn 11:45–57

Jesus says, "I tell the truth I heard from God"

Jesus said,
"If you obey my teaching,
you . . . will know the truth,
and the truth will set you free. . . .
[I] tell you the truth I heard from God,
yet you are trying to kill me."   John 8:31–32, 40

In the movie *How Green Was My Valley,*
a disillusioned pastor pours out his heart
to his congregation, saying,
"I thought when I was a young man
that I would conquer the world with truth.
Thought I would lead an army
greater than Alexander ever dreamed of,
not to conquer nations
but to liberate mankind—
but only a few of them heard.
Only a few of you understood."
Jesus poured out
his heart in a similar way near the end
of his ministry on earth.
For many Jews had closed their eyes to
his miracles and their ears to his message.

How open are my eyes and ears
to Jesus' miracles and message?
How faithfully do I try to follow Jesus?

Do not have Jesus Christ on your lips
and the world in your heart.
Saint Ignatius of Antioch (first century)

Journal

_____

_____

_____

_____

_____

_____

_____

_____

_____

_____

_____

_____

_____

Jesus says, "Prophets are not accepted by their own"

Jesus said,
"A prophet is respected everywhere except
in his hometown and by his own family."
Matthew 13:57

There's a moving Ray Bradbury story
about a little girl named Margot.
If memory serves me, she's part of an "Earth
colony" on a planet where it rains nonstop—
except for seven minutes every seven years.
Margot loved the sun and was excited
beyond belief when the "sun" day came.
That day, the other school kids (who doubted
the sun would shine) started teasing her.
During recess, they jokingly locked her
in a closet. Seconds later, the rain stopped
and the sun came out.
For seven delirious minutes the kids danced
and sang joyfully. Then the clouds closed,
the sun vanished, and the rain fell again.
Suddenly the children remembered Margot.
They unlocked the closet and let her out.

Why is it that "prophets" are often rejected
by others—and often deprived
of enjoying the fruit of their labor?

The Don Quixote of one generation
may live to hear himself called
the savior of society by the next.
James Russell Lowell

Jesus says, "If you won't believe me, believe my deeds"

*[The more Jesus preached, the more
the religious leaders rejected him.
Finally, Jesus said in desperation,]
"Even though you do not believe me,
you should at least believe my deeds."*
John 10:38

Violinist Fritz Kreisler was in Germany
with an hour to spare before leaving
for a concert in London.
He walked into a nearby music store.
The store owner eyed him suspiciously—
and especially his violin case.
Then the owner disappeared
and returned with two policemen.
They arrested Kreisler, saying,
"You have Fritz Kreisler's violin."
"I am Fritz Kreisler," he said.
"You can't pull that on us!" said the police.
Kreisler thought a moment.
Then he requested permission to play.
Although the police didn't believe his words,
they could not doubt his beautiful playing.

Jesus tried to lead his hearers
to a similar conclusion—but couldn't.
What lesson might the stories of Jesus and
Kreisler contain for me, personally?

*People may doubt what you say,
but they will believe what you do.*   Lewis Cass

Journal

Journal

Jesus speaks God's truth clearly and forthrightly

[One day someone said to Jesus,]
"Teacher, we know that you tell the truth,
without worrying about what people think.
You pay no attention to anyone's status,
but teach the truth about God."   Mark 12:14

Maurice Baring used to tell this story
to make a point clearly and forthrightly.
Two doctors were discussing medicine.
At one point the one said to the other,
"I'd like your opinion about a pregnancy.
This is not a hypothetical case,
but an actual historical case.
The pregnant mother has tuberculosis;
the father is syphilitic. Their first child
was blind, the second died, the third
was deaf and dumb, the fourth had tuberculosis.
Would you have recommended
that the parents terminate this pregnancy?"
The doctor said, "Yes, I would."
The other doctor said,
"Then Beethoven would not have been born."

What point
is Maurice Baring making by this story?
How forthrightly do I speak God's truth?

Jesus said,
"If [my disciples] keep quiet,
the stones themselves will start shouting."
Luke 19:40

Jesus foretells
his suffering and death

*Jesus said, "I must go to Jerusalem
and suffer much. . . ."
Peter said, "God forbid it, Lord!" . . .
Jesus said, "If any of you
want to come with me,
you must forget yourself, carry your cross,
and follow me."* Matthew 16:21–22, 24

A moth collector saw the cocoon
of a rare moth attached to a twig.
He clipped it and brought it home.
As the days passed, he noticed movement
inside the cocoon, but no moth emerged.
So he slit the cocoon slightly
to make it easier for the moth to emerge.
The moth emerged, but to his dismay
it was sickly looking and soon died.
When he told a friend, the friend said,
"Nature has arranged it so that the moth
must struggle to break out of the cocoon.
It's this daily struggle that enables it
to develop its wings. When they're strong
enough to break the cocoon, they're strong
enough to fly. When you tried to help it,
you killed its chances to mature and fly."

How are Jesus' words and this story linked?
What motivates me to pick up my cross daily?

*Out of suffering have emerged
the strongest souls.* Edwin Hubbel Chapin

Journal

Jesus says, "Whoever follows me will never walk in darkness"

Jesus said, "Who is not for me
is really against me;
anyone who does not help me gather
is really scattering." Luke 11:23

British artist William Holman Hunt
created a popular painting in 1854.
It shows Jesus knocking at a door.
On his head is a crown of thorns,
and in his hand is a lantern.
The painting seems to have been inspired
by three Bible passages:
"I stand at the door and knock" (Revelation 3:20);
"Carry your cross, and follow me" (Mark 8:34);
"Whoever follows me will . . .
never walk in darkness" (John 8:12).
What made the painting especially popular
is that the door
at which Jesus stands and knocks
has no outside handle.
It can be opened only from the inside.

What important point was Hunt making
by omitting the door's outside handle?
How does all this apply to me?

"Listen! I stand at the door and knock;
if any hear my voice and open the door,
I will come into their house and eat
with them, and they will eat with me."
Revelation 3:20

Jesus' fate is sealed by the religious leaders

*[The High Priest Caiaphas said to the
solemn assembly of religious leaders,]
"It is better for you to have one man die
for the people, instead of having
the whole nation destroyed."* John 11:50

Ernest Gordon recalls this true story
from a Japanese prison camp in Thailand.
One day, when the shovels were counted
after work, the guard on duty went berserk.
He said one shovel was missing.
Screaming in broken English, he ordered
the thief to step up. When no one did,
he cocked his rifle and threatened to fire
into the group.
At this point, an Australian came forward.
The Aussie stood silently as the guard
beat him. Finally, the guard struck him
a thunderous blow with his rifle on the head.
The Aussie dropped—clearly dead,
but the guard kept beating him savagely.
Then the work crew carried the shovels
and the dead Aussie back to the guard house.
There the shovels were counted again.
No shovel was missing after all.

What are my thoughts as I imagine myself
to be the Aussie, before stepping forward?

*"The greatest love you can have for your friends
is to give your life for them."* John 15:13

Journal

Jesus gives himself

The Passover Festival was near.
People wondered if Jesus would go to Jerusalem
to celebrate it, because the authorities had
issued an order for his arrest.   John 11:55

Suddenly, all Jerusalem buzzed excitedly.
Jesus was approaching the city on a donkey.
The crowds cut palm branches
and greeted him, shouting,
"God bless him who comes
in the name of the Lord!"   Matthew 21:9

[After meeting with his apostles,
Jesus told Peter and John,]
"A man carrying a jar of water . . .
will show you a . . . room upstairs,
where you will get everything ready."

They went off and found everything
just as Jesus had told them,
and they prepared
the Passover meal.   Luke 22:10, 12–13

The Passover meal was eaten at night
after the appearance of the first stars,
so that all Jews began it together.

Jesus took his place at the table
with the apostles. He said to them,
"I have wanted so much
to eat this Passover meal with you
before I suffer!"   Luke 22:14–15

And so the final days of Jesus' life began.
This week's meditations focus on
the eventful Last Supper.

Prayer procedure

You may wish to add the following prayer
to the usual opening prayer
of your meditation.

Jesus, help me to open my heart
to whatever grace you want to give me
during this important meditation.

Suggested daily readings

1 Jesus washes the feet   Jn 13:1–17
2 Jesus foretells Judas' betrayal   Jn 13:21–30
3 Jesus begins the Passover meal   Lk 22:7–17
4 Jesus is the Bread of Life   Jn 6:25–48
5 Jesus gives eternal life   Jn 6:49–69
6 Jesus shares himself   Lk 22:19–20
7 Jesus prays for his disciples   Jn 17:1–26

Jesus washes the feet of the disciples

[After all were seated at table, Jesus rose and washed the feet of each, saying,]
"You do not understand now what I am doing, but you will understand later." John 13:7

An old poem goes something like this:
"Up in a quaint old attic,
as the raindrops pattered down,
I sat paging through an old schoolbook—
dusty, tattered, and brown.
I came to a page that was folded down.
Across it was written in childish hand:
'Teacher says to leave this for now,
'tis hard to understand.'
I unfolded the page and read.
Then I nodded my head and said,
'Teacher was right—now I understand.'
There are lots of pages in the book of life
that are hard to understand.
All we can do is fold them down and write:
'Teacher says to leave this for now,
'tis hard to understand.'
Then someday—maybe only in heaven—
we will unfold the pages again,
read them, and say, 'Teacher was right—
now I understand.'"
Retold from an unknown author

What is one thing I find hard to understand?

Trust in the Lord with all your heart. Proverbs 3:5

Journal

Journal

_____

_____

_____

_____

_____

_____

_____

_____

_____

_____

_____

_____

Jesus foretells betrayal by Judas

[Following the washing of feet,
Jesus sat down and said,]
"One of you is going to betray me."   John 13:21

An old poem reads:
"I watched them tear a building down,
A gang of men in a busy town.
With a mighty heave and lusty yell,
They swung a beam and a side wall fell.
I said to the foreman,
'Are these men as skilled
As the men you'd hire if you had to build?'
He laughed and said, 'No indeed!
Just a common laborer is all I need.
And I can wreck in a day or two
What it took the builder a year to do.'
And I thought to myself as I went my way,
'Just which of these roles have I tried to play?
Am I a builder who works with care,
Measuring life by the rule and square,
Or am I a wrecker as I walk the town,
Content with the labor of tearing down?' "
Author unknown

When it comes to God's Kingdom,
what evidence suggests I am a builder
who works with care, not a wrecker
who tears down?

Judas Iscariot . . . went off to the chief priests
in order to betray Jesus.   Mark 14:10

Jesus begins
the Passover meal

*Then Jesus took a cup, gave thanks to God,
and said, "Take this and share it."* Luke 22:17

Jesus introduced the Passover meal
with the pre-meal cup of red wine.
Sharing the same "cup" dramatizes
the unity of all present; red wine recalls
both the blood-marked doors in Egypt and
the covenant blood at Mount Sinai.
The meal begins with the eating of bitter herbs,
which cues the youngest to ask,
"Why is this meal different?"
The father then explains the symbolic foods.
Bitter herbs recall Israel's years of bitter slavery
in Egypt. *Clay-colored sauce* recalls making
clay bricks under the hot sun.
Unleavened bread recalls Israel's swift exit
from Egypt—not even waiting
for the next day's bread to rise.
The *lamb* recalls both the *sacrificial blood*
that the Hebrews smeared on their doorposts
to save them from the "angel of death" and
the *sacrificial flesh* that nourished them as they
set out on their journey to freedom. Exodus 12

How does the lamb symbolism prepare me
for what the "Lamb of God" is about to do?

*The Baptist said, "There is the Lamb of God,
who takes away the sin of the world! . . .
He is the Son of God."* John 1:29, 34

Jesus gives himself to us as our spiritual food

Jesus took . . . bread,
gave thanks to God, broke it,
and gave it to his disciples, saying,
"This is my body, which is given for you.
Do this in memory of me." Luke 22:19

After the eating of the bitter herbs,
a reverent silence fell upon the disciples
as Jesus took bread in his hands
and said, "This is my body."
The words recall the day in the synagogue
at Capernaum when Jesus said,
"I am the living bread
that came down from heaven.
If you eat this bread,
you will live forever.
The bread that I will give . . . is my flesh . . .
that the world may live." John 6:51
The words also recall that after Jesus
spoke these words, many people grumbled,
" 'This teaching is too hard.
Who can listen to it?' . . .
Because of this, many of Jesus' followers
turned back and would not go with him
any more." John 6:60, 66

How do I feel about Jesus' words and why?

The bread we break: when we eat it,
we are sharing in the body of Christ.
1 Corinthians 10:16

Journal

Jesus gives himself to us as our spiritual drink

Journal

*Jesus gave his disciples the cup
after the supper, saying, "This cup is God's
new covenant sealed with my blood,
which is poured out for you."*   Luke 22:20

Passover meals end with a cup of wine.
Once again, as Jesus prepared the wine,
a silence fell over the disciples.
Then Jesus said,
"This cup is God's new covenant
sealed with my blood."
The phrase "new covenant" recalls
God's promise to the prophet Jeremiah:
"The time is coming
when I will make a new covenant
with the people of Israel."   Jeremiah 31:31
The phrase "sealed with my blood"
recalls the words of the old covenant:
"This is the blood
that seals the covenant
which the LORD made with you."   Exodus 24:8

In my imagination, I sit across from Jesus,
taking to heart everything he says.
What are my thoughts as I ponder his words?

*The cup we use in the Lord's Supper
and for which we give thanks to God:
when we drink from it,
we are sharing in the blood of Christ.*
1 Corinthians 10:16

Journal

_____

_____

_____

_____

_____

_____

_____

_____

_____

_____

_____

Jesus concludes
the Last Supper

*[All Passover meals end with the singing
of the Hallel. Its words include:]
"The stone which the builders rejected
as worthless turned out to be
the most important of all.
This was done by the Lord;
what a wonderful sight it is!"*   Matthew 21:42

Jesus recalled these words of the Hallel
in his parable of the vineyard tenants.
In that parable, the vineyard owner (God)
sends his "dear son" to tenants.
They respond by killing him.
How appropriate these words were as Jesus
sang them on this particular night:
"I am your servant, LORD. . . .
I will not die; instead, I will live. . . .
The stone which the builders rejected
as worthless turned out to be
the most important of all.
This was done by the LORD;
what a wonderful sight it is!"
Psalms 116:16; 118:17, 22–23

These words from the Hallel invite me
to pause after each sentence and meditate.
How do they apply in a special way to Jesus?

*This is the day of the LORD's victory;
let us be happy, let us celebrate!*
                                Psalms 118:24

Jesus and his disciples
go to the Mount of Olives

[After the singing of the Hallel,]
Jesus and his disciples went out
to the Mount of Olives.   Mark 14:26

The disciples' hearts must have been filled
with joy as they walked along under the stars
with Jesus to the Mount of Olives.
But Jesus had said too many
sorrow-shadowed things during the supper
to allow for unrestrained joy.
For example, he said, "This is my body,
which is *given* for you."
"This is my blood,
which is *poured out* for you."
Jesus had warned his disciples
that he was to die violently (Matthew 16:21),
but they never quite got the point.
Perhaps now they began to understand.

What are my thoughts as I reflect upon
Jesus' gift of himself at the Last Supper?

Astronauts Aldrin and Armstrong
had just landed on the moon.
While Armstrong prepared for his moon walk,
Aldrin unpacked bread and wine. He writes:
"I poured the wine into the chalice. . . .
It was interesting to think that the very first liquid
ever poured on the moon and the first food
eaten there were communion elements.
                    Guideposts Treasury of Faith

Jesus is crucified

The Mount of Olives
overlooks the walled city of Jerusalem.
On its lower slopes
stands a cluster of eight old olive trees.
Nobody knows how old the trees are.
An ancient Roman historian says that
people believed olive trees lived forever.

The belief probably grew out of the fact
that old olive trees often generated shoots.
These shoots then grew into young trees.
Eventually the parent tree died,
leaving the young trees to carry on
where the parent tree left off.

It may well be, therefore,
that the eight old olive trees
mark the exact spot
where Jesus and his disciples went
after the Last Supper.

The distance to the mount
from the Last Supper room
was probably a little over a mile.
The little group
probably walked much of the distance
that Passover night in prayerful silence.

Their destination was a small orchard
on the lower slopes,
called the garden of Gethsemane.

The word *Gethsemane* means "olive press."
This suggests that the garden housed
a stone press for crushing oil from olives.
It was in this small garden that Jesus began
the final days of his life on earth.

Prayer procedure

Once again, after saying
the usual opening prayer before meditation,
you might wish to add this brief prayer:

*Loving God, help me to open my heart fully
to whatever grace you want to give me
as I meditate on your Son's death for me.*

Suggested daily readings

1	Jesus is arrested	Lk 22:39–53
2	Jesus is sentenced to death	Lk 23:1–25
3	Jesus is crucified	Lk 23:26–43
4	Jesus' side is pierced	Jn 19:31–37
5	Jesus dies on the cross	Jn 19:25–30
6	Jesus is Lord	Phil 2:1–11
7	Jesus is buried	Lk 23:50–56

Jesus goes off alone
and prays

[At Gethsemane, Jesus went off alone,]
and knelt down and prayed,
"Father, if you will, take this cup of suffering
away from me. Not my will, however,
but your will be done."   Luke 22:41–42

As Jesus finished praying, Judas arrived
with an armed crowd.   Matthew 26:47
He went up to Jesus and kissed him.
Jesus said, "Judas, is it with a kiss
that you betray the Son of Man?"   Luke 22:48
The disciples scuffled briefly
with the soldiers and then fled.   Mark 14:45–50
Jesus was then taken to the high priest.
After the hearing, he was jailed for the night.

I imagine myself to be one of the following:
Peter, Judas, Jesus. What are my thoughts
as I lie in bed this night, unable to sleep?

A pianist said of Chopin's nocturne
in C sharp minor: "All is trouble,
until the person in the piece talks with God.
Then peace comes."
The same thing is true of Jesus.
He went into Gethsemane in the dark;
he came out in the light—
because he talked with God.
He went into Gethsemane in agony;
he came out with peace in his soul—
because he talked with God.   William Barclay

Journal

Journal

Jesus is condemned and maltreated

[The next day, the Jewish High Council took Jesus before Pilate. After listening to their accusations, Pilate said,] "I cannot find anything he has done to deserve death! I will have him whipped and set him free." But they kept on shouting. . . . So Pilate passed the sentence on Jesus that they were asking for. Luke 23:22–24

England's Dr. Sheila Cassidy worked among the very poor in Chile in the 1970s. One day she treated a wounded man who could not go to a hospital for fear of the corrupt secret police. She was informed upon, arrested, and tortured for days to get her to divulge information. She says: "For the first time in my life I thought I was going to die. . . . I was experiencing in some slight way what Christ had suffered. . . . I suddenly felt enormously loved by God . . . because I felt I had in a way participated in his suffering."

What are my thoughts as I imagine myself to be Cassidy suffering for helping the poor? What may have been Jesus' thoughts after being condemned for my sins?

The LORD says, "I have swept your sins away like a cloud. Come back to me." Isaiah 44:21–22

Jesus forgives those who crucify him

The soldiers led Jesus away. . . .
When they came to the place called
"The Skull," they crucified Jesus there,
and the two criminals, one on his right
and the other on his left.
Jesus said, "Forgive them, Father!
They don't know what they are doing."
Luke 23:26, 33–34

The movie *The Ox-Bow Incident*
concerns town leaders who bypass the law
and hang three people without a trial.
Later they learn the terrible truth.
The three people were innocent.
Before being hanged, one young man
asks to write a letter to his young wife.
After he is hanged, someone reads it.
A portion of it says:
"I suppose there's some good men
[in this crowd] . . . only they don't realize
what they're doing. They're the ones
I feel sorry for, 'cause it'll be over for me
in a little while, but they'll have to go on
remembering the rest of their lives."

What strikes me most about the attitudes
of Jesus and the young man? What would
probably have been my own attitude?

It wasn't the nails that held Jesus on the cross
but his love for us.   Anonymous

Journal

155

Journal

Jesus' side is pierced by the soldier

One of the soldiers . . . plunged his spear into Jesus' side, and at once blood and water poured out.   John 19:34

A woman missionary visited
the tent of an Arab youth who was dying.
She asked if she might tell him a story.
When the mother nodded, the woman knelt
and told him how Jesus died on the cross
for people's wrong-doing.
The youth's eyes showed unusual interest.
The missionary returned the next day
and told him the same story.
Now his face reflected peace and love.
The missionary returned again the next day
and started telling him about Jesus' birth.
But he raised his hand and said, "No! Not that!
Tell me again how he died for us."
When the missionary returned the fourth day,
the boy's mother was weeping.
Her son had died. She told the missionary
that just before he died, someone began
reading prayers to him. But he raised his hand
and said feebly, "No! Not that!
Tell me how Jesus died for my sins."

Why do I think the story of Jesus' death
had such a powerful impact on the youth?

*Nothing in my hand I bring.
Simply to the cross I cling.*   August Toplady

Jesus "was really the Son of God"

The army officer who was standing there in front of the cross saw how Jesus had died. "This man was really the Son of God!" he said. Mark 15:39

The apostle John
was standing in front of the cross
not far from the army officer.
John would later sum all of Scripture
in one line:
"God loved the world so much
that he gave his only Son,
so that everyone who believes in him
may not die but have eternal life." John 3:16
And so, in God's providence,
a pagan Roman army officer becomes
the first in a long line of believers.

What tends to keep me from saying
what the army officer did?
How do I explain this tendency?

*The suffering of the cross
is not meant for itself. . . .
Christ does not suffer
because suffering is in itself a value. . . .
It is not a love for suffering . . .
which Christ reveals,
but the love of Jesus for us
even unto death.*
Anthony Padovano, *Who Is Christ?*

Journal

_____

_____

_____

_____

_____

_____

_____

_____

_____

_____

_____

Jesus' death on the cross gave life to many people

"The Son of Man . . . came . . . to give his life to redeem many people."   Mark 10:45

Someone asked an old chief,
"Why are you always talking about Jesus?"
The chief didn't say anything.
Instead, he collected some dry grass
and twigs and arranged them in a circle.
Next he caught a caterpillar,
feeding on a nearby clump of weeds.
He placed it inside the circle.
Then he took a match and set fire
to the dry grass and the twigs.
As the fire blazed up, the caterpillar
began to search for an escape.
At this point the old chief
extended his finger to the caterpillar.
Instantly, it climbed onto it.
The chief said,
"That's what Jesus did for me.
I was like the caterpillar—
confused, frightened, without hope.
Then Jesus rescued me.
How can I not talk about my savior
and praise him for his love and mercy?"

How grateful am I for what Jesus has done
for me, and how do I show it concretely?

*There is a sense in which no gift is ours
till we have thanked the giver.*   E. C. McKenzie

Jesus is buried
in a tomb cut from rock

*[After Jesus died, Joseph of Arimathea]
took the body . . . and placed it in a tomb
which had been dug out of solid rock.
Then he rolled a large stone across
the entrance to the tomb.*   Mark 15:46

In the book *Peter Calvey: Hermit,*
a young person comes to an old monk
to learn how to meditate. The monk says:
"Go back in your imagination
and make yourself present at the event.
Stand beneath the cross of Jesus.
Through the eyes of your imagination,
see everything as it happens.
With the ears of your imagination,
hear everything that is spoken."
Before the monk could finish, however,
the young person interrupts, saying,
"But isn't that method of meditation
out of date these days?" The monk replies,
"No method of meditation is out of date
if it helps us re-create the genuine spirit
of the Gospels and leads us
to a deeper knowledge and love of Jesus."

In my imagination, I watch Jesus being
taken down from the cross and buried.
What are my thoughts?

*"The greatest love you can have for your friends
is to give your life for them."*   John 15:13

Jesus is raised

It was possible in Jesus' day to deify
someone in almost every nation on earth.
There was one place, however,
where this was absolutely impossible.
That was in Israel.

Jews believed in only one God.
That's why they had only one Temple.

Jews also honored Abraham and Moses,
but they would rather have died
than think these men might be
God or God's only Son.

Yet three days after Jesus' crucifixion,
his distraught, defeated disciples
were amazingly transformed.

They set out fearlessly
to tell the whole world the "good news."
"Jesus is risen! Jesus is risen!"

So passionate was their belief
that they would have gladly suffered
and died for it.

Had they been deluded or dishonest
about their belief,
certainly one or more of the eleven
would have confessed this
under the pressure of death.
But none did!

Their witness never wavered.
Rather, they experienced an amazing power
that even enabled them to work miracles!

The lives and message of these men
changed the course of human history.
No reasonable explanation
has ever been given to account for
their transformed lives
except their own:
they had seen Jesus alive.
Robert L. Cleath, *Christianity Today*

This week's meditations focus on
the central message of Christianity:
Jesus' resurrection from the dead.

Suggested daily readings

1	Jesus is risen	Mt 28:1–10
2	Jesus appears to Magdalene	Jn 20: 11–18
3	Peter and John believe	Jn 20: 1–10
4	Jesus appears to two disciples	Lk 24:13–27
5	Jesus reveals himself	Lk 24: 28–35
6	Jesus' resurrection is denied	Mt 28:11–15
7	Jesus appears to his disciples	Jn 20:19–29

"Jesus is not here," said the angel; "he is risen!"

Journal

*[Sunday morning some women went
to the tomb. Suddenly the earth quaked.]
An angel . . . spoke . . .
"I know you are looking for Jesus,
who was crucified. He is not here;
he has been raised."* Matthew 28:2, 5–6

Years ago, a man was looking at a painting
of the Crucifixion in a shop window.
Suddenly a little boy appeared and said,
"That's Jesus on the cross, sir.
They nailed him there.
That lady there is his mother.
She's looking at what they did.
When Jesus died, sir, they buried him—
over there by the edge of the picture."
The boy's faith
moved the man so much he couldn't speak.
He patted the boy's shoulder and walked on.
Suddenly the boy appeared again.
"I forgot to tell you, sir. It's okay! It's okay!
Because Jesus rose!"

How can I make Jesus' death and resurrection
as alive for me
as it was for the boy?

*Universe / and every universe beyond, /
spin and blaze, / whirl and dance, /
leap and laugh / as never before. . . . /
Christ has smashed death.* Norman Habel

Journal

Jesus sends Magdalene to the disciples

[Jesus said to Mary Magdalene,
"Go to my disciples] and tell them
that I am returning to . . .
my God and their God."   John 20:17

Caryll Houselander writes:
"I was in an underground train,
a crowded train in which
all sorts of people jostled together . . .
going home at the end of the day.
Quite suddenly I saw in my mind,
but as vividly as a wonderful picture,
Christ in them all . . .
living in them, dying in them,
rejoicing in them, sorrowing in them. . . .
I came out into the street
and walked a long time in the crowds.
It was the same thing here,
on every side, in every passerby—Christ."
A Rocking-Horse Catholic

To what extent and how
do I experience the risen Jesus
present in our world—
filling it and everyone
with his truth and his power?

Jesus' power working in us
is able to do so much more
than we can ever ask for,
or even think of.   Ephesians 3:20

Jesus' disciples go to the tomb, see, and believe

[Mary Magdalene ran to tell the "good news"]
to Simon Peter and the other disciple,
whom Jesus loved. . . . Then Peter and
the other disciple went to the tomb . . .
saw and believed.   John 20:2–3, 8

Mary Helen Gee says,
"When my kids were small,
I kept two sets of nativity figures:
an expensive set on the mantle
and a cheap set under the tree,
for the kids to play with—even take to bed
because 'Baby Jesus got cold during the night.'"
Jesus did something not too unlike this
in the course of his own life on earth.
On Christmas morning
he revealed his human side
and invited us to relate to him
as our friend and companion.
On Easter morning
he revealed his divine side
and invited us to relate to him
as our Lord and Savior.

What do I find most attractive
about Jesus in his human nature?
His divine nature?

Jesus is
the condescension of divinity,
and the exaltation of humanity.   Phillips Brooks

Journal

Jesus appears
to two Emmaus disciples

[Two disciples were returning to Emmaus,
unaware that Jesus had risen.
Suddenly Jesus came alongside them,
but they didn't recognize him.
After listening to their sad story,
Jesus said,] "How foolish you are,
how slow you are to believe everything
the prophets said! Was is not necessary
for the Messiah to suffer these things
and then to enter his glory?"   Luke 24:25–26

Noreen Towers worked hard among
the poor, but with no evident results.
One night she went to bed—planning to quit.
The next morning, shortly after she awoke,
something happened.
It was as if Jesus himself said to her,
"Can you not trust my plan for you?"
She writes: "Then I realized
that I did not have to see the plan;
I only had to trust him. I arose from my bed
a different person." She had gone to bed
"a broken, defeated person" and arose
"a person with unshakable hope and faith."
International Christian Digest

When was I closest to being "a broken,
defeated person"? What kept me going?

How else but through a broken heart
May the Lord Christ enter in?   Oscar Wilde

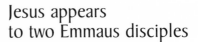

Jesus is recognized in the breaking of the bread

[When the two disciples reached Emmaus,
they said to Jesus, whom they still
did not recognize,] "Stay with us. . . ."
So he went in to stay with them. . . .
[And they] recognized the Lord
when he broke the bread.   Luke 24:29, 35

After meditating on this Emmaus story
someone wrote: "Lord Jesus, look with love
on those of us who have left you behind
in some distant, unmarked tomb.
Seek us out as you did the two disciples
on the road to Emmaus.
Walk along beside us and explain
the Scriptures to us, as you did to them.
Fan to flame the dying embers of our faith,
and make our hearts burn again within us.
Come into our house and sit at table with us.
Take into your hands our humble bread.
Bless it and fill it with your risen presence.
Then break it
and release the blindness of our eyes
that we may also recognize you
in all your risen glory."   M. L.

What seems to be the message of the
"breaking of the bread" and the recognition
of the risen Jesus in that action?
What might it be saying to me, personally?

"Do this in memory of me."   Luke 22:19

Journal

Jesus defeats death; truth is victorious

[During his lifetime,]
Jesus said to those who believed in him,
". . . You will know the truth,
and the truth will set you free."   John 8:31–32

In John Masefield's *The Trial of Jesus,*
the following conversation takes place
between Pilate's wife and the centurion
who stood beneath the cross of Jesus:
"Do you think he is dead?"
"No lady, I don't."
"Then where is he?"
"Let loose in the world, lady,
where neither Roman nor Jew
can stop his truth."
The truth is Jesus is victorious over death.
The truth is Jesus wants to share
his victory with us—if we but let him.
The truth is Jesus wants to work
Easter miracles through us.
The truth is nothing has the power
to hold us hostage anymore—not pain,
not sorrow, not sin, not even death.

What keeps me from letting Jesus
share his victory with me fully
and work Easter miracles through me?

He has freed the universe.
You and I and everything are free again,
new again, alive again.   Norman Habel

Jesus gives new life to all who believe in him

These [things] have been written
in order that you may believe
that Jesus is the Messiah,
the Son of God,
and that through your faith in him
you may have life.   John 20:31

One August afternoon, Darryl Stingley
of the New England Patriots was savagely hit
by Jack Tatum of the Oakland Raiders.
He was left paralyzed from the chest down.
Today Darryl can use only one hand
and is confined to a wheelchair.
But he insists that in some ways
his life is better now than before, saying,
"I had tunnel vision in my playing days.
All I wanted was
to be the best athlete I could,
and a lot of things were overlooked.
Now I've come back to them.
This is a rebirth for me.
Not only physically but spiritually. . . .
I really have a lot more meaning and purpose
to live for now than ever before."

Stingley's death and rebirth happened,
also, to the early Christian community.
How can I share in it 2,000 years later?

If we share Christ's suffering,
we will also share his glory.   Romans 8:17

The Spirit comes

The religious leaders
thought Jesus' death would put an end to
his teaching and the spread of Christianity.
Just the opposite was true.

On Easter Sunday night,
the disciples were gathered together.
Suddenly Jesus appeared and said:

"Peace be with you.
As the Father sent me, so I send you."
Then he breathed on them and said,
"Receive the Holy Spirit."   John 20:21–22

Luke tells the rest of the story. He writes:

In my first book I wrote about all
the things that Jesus did and taught
from the time he began his work
until the day he was taken up to heaven. . . .

For forty days after his death
he appeared to his apostles . . .
and he talked with them
about the Kingdom of God. . . .
He gave them this order:
"Do not leave Jerusalem. . . .
In a few days you will be baptized
with the Holy Spirit. . . .
You will be filled with power,
and you will be witnesses for me . . .
to the ends of the earth."   Acts 1:1–5, 8

Then came the final fulfillment
of Jesus' promise.
On Pentecost the Holy Spirit
came upon the entire Christian community:

Suddenly there was a noise . . .
like a strong wind blowing. . . .
They were all filled with the Holy Spirit.
                                    Acts 2:2, 4

This week's meditations deal with
the coming of the promised Holy Spirit.

Suggested daily readings

1 Jesus makes a promise   Jn 14:1–14
2 Jesus promises the Spirit   Jn 16:1–11
3 Jesus details the Spirit's work Jn 16:12–15
4 Jesus makes another promise   Jn 16:16–20
5 Jesus makes a further promise   Jn 16:21–24
6 Jesus sends the Spirit   Jn 20:19–29
7 Jesus did many other things   Jn 21:25

Jesus said, "I am going to prepare a place for you"

[Jesus said to his disciples,] "I am going to prepare a place for you." John 14:2

Grub worms at the bottom of a pond
couldn't understand why those
who climbed up the stems of the water lilies
never returned to tell them what they found.
They agreed that the next one to climb up
should return to tell them what it found.
One day the leader of the grubs decided
to climb up the stem.
When he reached the top, he was astounded.
Everything was fantastically beautiful.
Even more astounding
is what then happened to him.
He changed into a gorgeous dragonfly.
As he circled the pond,
peering down at his friends under the water,
he couldn't figure out how to return to them.
Then he realized that even if he did get back,
his friends would never recognize him.

How is this story like one of Jesus' parables?
What might it be saying to me, personally?

From the voiceless lips
of the unreplying dead there comes no word.
But in the night of Death,
Hope sees a star, and listening Love
can hear the rustle of a wing.
Robert Green Ingersoll

Journal

_____

_____

_____

_____

_____

_____

_____

_____

_____

_____

_____

_____

_____

The Holy Spirit
will come to you

Jesus said, "It is better for you that I go away, because if I do not go, the Helper [Holy Spirit] will not come to you." John 16:7

During the religious oppression in China in the 1950s, a small child named Mei was in prison with her Christian mother. She had a remarkable faith and believed that the Spirit comes to all Christians much as the Bible says:
"Peter and John
placed their hands on [the believers], and they received the Holy Spirit." Acts 8:17
And so she requested
and received the Holy Spirit in this way. Meanwhile, unsuspecting Chinese guards let Mei run freely throughout the prison. When Christians outside the prison found a way to smuggle Communion to prisoners, it was Mei who gave it to them—
even those in solitary confinement. She said, "I'm not afraid; the Spirit is within me." From a report by F. Steels

How do I experience the Spirit's presence in my everyday life?

The Spirit produces love, joy, peace, patience, kindness, goodness, faithfulness, humility, and self-control.
Galatians 5:22–23

The Spirit will lead you further into all truth

[Jesus told his disciples,]
"I have much more to tell you, but now
it would be too much for you to bear.
When, however, the Spirit comes,
who reveals the truth about God,
he will lead you into all the truth."

John 16:12–13

Lincoln had bad news for his Cabinet.
He introduced it by telling this story.
A worker came to a farmer with the news,
"One of your team of oxen dropped dead."
The farmer stood silently for a moment.
Then before he could say anything,
the worker said, "The other oxen died too."
When the farmer regained his composure,
he said, "Why didn't you tell me right away
that both of my oxen were dead?"
The worker said, "I didn't want to tell you
too much at one time. I was afraid
it might be too much for you to bear."

Jesus' words and Lincoln's story invite me
to reflect that some things can't be rushed,
the aging of wine, for instance.
What message might this hold for me
right now in my own life?

Everything that happens in this world
happens at the time God chooses.

Ecclesiastes 3:1

Journal

"When the Spirit comes, you will speak about me"

*Jesus said,
"I will send the Holy Spirit to you. . . .
And you . . . will speak about me."*

John 15:26–27

In a scene in the film *Network,*
Peter Finch explains his "calling"
to speak the truth to his TV audience:
"The voice said to me,
'I want you to tell the people the truth,
not an easy thing to do, because
the people don't want to know the truth.'
And I said, 'You're kidding.
What the hell should I know about truth?'
But the voice said to me,
'Don't worry about the truth.
I will put the words in your mouth.'
And I said,
'What is this, the burning bush? . . .
I'm not Moses.'"
Possibly Jesus' disciples felt the same way
when Jesus promised to send the Spirit
to help them preach the "good news"
of God's Kingdom to the entire world.

Where and how do I encounter
the Holy Spirit working in my life
or elsewhere in today's world?

*O Holy Spirit, Paraclete, perfect in us
the work begun by Jesus.* Pope John XXIII

Jesus said, "What you ask in my name you'll receive"

*[Jesus said, "When I ascend to heaven,]
the Father will give you whatever you
ask of him in my name."*   John 16:23

A child wrote
his description of Jesus for his teacher:
"Jesus is God's Son.
He used to do all the hard work,
like walking on water and doing miracles,
and trying to teach people—
who didn't want to learn. . . .
They finally got tired
of him preaching and crucified him.
But he was good and kind like his Father
and he told his Father . . . to forgive them. . . .
His Dad (God) . . . told him he didn't have
to go out on the road any more.
And now Jesus helps his Dad by listening
to prayers and seeing which ones
are important for God to take care of and
which ones he can take care of himself."

Why is it that kids
often grasp the great truths of faith
so simply and correctly?
How confidently do I pray to Jesus,
risen and reigning in glory in heaven?

*Jesus impacted the lives
of his followers more powerfully
after his death than before it.*   Anonymous

Journal

Journal

Jesus gives the Spirit to his disciples

[Jesus breathed on his disciples and said,] "Receive the Holy Spirit." John 20:22

Jesus likened the Spirit to water. John 7:38
"Water descends from heaven as rain.
It is always the same, but it produces
different effects in different things:
one in the palm tree, another in the vine. . . .
It adapts to each creature." Saint Cyril
It is the same with the Spirit. Paul writes:
"No one can confess 'Jesus is Lord,'
without being guided by the Holy Spirit.
There are different kinds of spiritual gifts,
but the same Spirit gives them.
There are different ways of serving,
but the same Lord is served. . . .
The Spirit's presence is shown in some way
in each person for the good of all."
1 Corinthians 12:3–5, 7

How does the Spirit of Jesus impact me?

The Spirit gives me:
new eyes to see the face of Jesus
in all who stand in need,
new ears to hear the voice of Jesus
in all who cry to heaven for justice,
a new tongue to tell the message of Jesus
to all who have never heard it,
a new heart to share the love of Jesus
with all who have never experienced it.

Jesus will return
and fill us with gladness

[Jesus promised to return, saying,]
"I will see you again, and
your hearts will be filled with gladness,
the kind of gladness that no one
can take away from you." John 16:22

The 50-year-old film *It's a Wonderful Life*
grew out of a parable on a Christmas card.
It's about a man
who thought his life was a total failure.
One day an angel appeared and showed him
how his life impacted the lives of hundreds
of people. The man was stunned and filled
with gladness at what he saw.
In the 1990s, computers colored
the 50-year-old black-and-white film,
erased the static from its soundtrack, and
transformed it into an even greater film.

It's a Wonderful Life is a kind of parable
of my own life. Jesus has called me
and gifted me with the Holy Spirit to impact
all whom I meet in life. He has done more!
He has promised that he will return,
fill me with gladness, and transform me
beyond anything I ever dreamed possible.

If seeds in the black earth
can turn into such beautiful roses,
what might the heart of man become
in its long journey to the stars? G. K. Chesterton

Other Books in this Series

HOLY SPIRIT: Meditations for the Millennium
GOD the FATHER: Meditations for the Millennium

Other Books by Mark Link

Bible 2000

Challenge 2000

Vision 2000

Mission 2000

Action 2000

For further information call or write:

Thomas More®
An RCL Company
200 East Bethany Drive
Allen, Texas 75002–3804

Toll Free   800–264–0368
Fax   800–688–8356

Daily Meditation Format

| *Begin each meditation with this prayer:* |

Father, you created me
and put me on earth for a purpose.
Jesus, you died for me
and called me to complete your work.
Holy Spirit, you help me
to carry out the work
for which I was created and called.
In your presence and name—
Father, Son, and Holy Spirit—
I begin my meditation.
May all my thoughts and inspirations
have their origin in you
and be directed to your glory.

| *Follow this format for each meditation:* |

1. READ the meditation prayerfully.
   (About one minute.)
2. THINK about what struck you most
   as you read the meditation. Why this?
   (About four minutes.)
3. SPEAK to God about your thoughts.
   (About one minute.)
4. LISTEN to God's response.
   Simply rest in God's presence
   with an open mind and an open heart.
   (About four minutes.)
5. END each meditation by praying the
   Lord's Prayer slowly and reverently.